IN VARIOUS DIRECTIONS

TYRONE GUTHRIE

In Various Directions

A VIEW OF THEATRE

THE MACMILLAN COMPANY, NEW YORK

COLLIER-MACMILLAN LIMITED, LONDON

ACKNOWLEDGMENTS

Some of the material in this book originally appeared in the New York *Times*. The sections on *Julius Caesar, The Merchant of Venice* and *The Tempest* are reprinted by permission from SHAKESPEARE: TEN GREAT PLAYS. Introduction and commentaries by Sir Tyrone Guthrie. Copyright © 1962 by Golden Press, Inc. The section on *Coriolanus* is from the Laurel Shakespeare edition of CORIOLANUS, reprinted by permission of Dell Publishing Company, Inc. "Theatre and Television" is from THE EIGHTH ART. Copyright © 1962 by Holt, Rinehart & Winston, Inc.

Second Printing 1966

The Macmillan Company, New York
Collier-Macmillan Canada Ltd., Toronto, Ontario

Library of Congress Catalog Number: 65-26729

Printed in the United States of America

Contents

CONTENTS

List of Illustrations
(facing page 96)

Foreword

THOUGH MY TIME and energies have been principally spent in the theatre, which has also been the principal source of my livelihood, I have through the years tried to clarify my ideas and also to supplement my income by writing. It has always surprised and pleased me that anyone should want to share my experiences and impressions by reading them; and it has been even more surprising and pleasing that publishers should be willing to pay me for what, though it is hard work, is really a pleasure, indeed an addiction.

This book consists of a series of pieces which its publisher thinks might be worthy to appear in a less ephemeral form than hitherto; he also believes that they add up to some coherent statement of A Point of View. I am less confident on both scores, but very grateful to the New York *Times,* the B.B.C., Telefis Eireann, Golden Books, Dell Books, Holt, Rinehart and Winston, Inc., who have given permission to use or reprint material which at different times they commissioned. (*The Eighth Art,* in which "Theatre versus Television" appears, was published by Holt, Rinehart and Winston but commissioned by C.B.S.)

Much of what is included in this book was first presented over radio and television and has never before appeared in print, and a number of articles were written especially for this book.

T. G.

1. SELF-PORTRAIT

I SUPPOSE no one can present his own portrait quite without bias. Unless you're a very perverse kind of being you want to make a good impression, so you tone down the less admirable features of your own character and highlight what you hope people may like.

But haven't you noticed? As soon as people see that you're sitting up and begging to be loved, they just *hate* you. Winsomeness becomes a boomerang and knocks you flat.

No, I shall not attempt any endearing young charms. I'll try to stick to facts.

I was born in 1900. Married. No children. I live in County Monaghan, Ireland, between Newbliss and Cootehill. Our home, Annagh-ma-Kerrig, is a sort of cross between a big farmhouse and a small big house. My mother's great-grandfather bought it nearly two hundred years ago. He was a local doctor, who had made some money. From the name—Moorhead—I imagine that the family had come sometime from the south of Scotland.

Tyrone Power, an Irish actor of the early nineteenth century, was the great-grandfather of the film star. He was my great-grandfather too. His son, also called Tyrone Power, was in the British army. In the eighteen forties he was stationed at Cootehill, in County Cavan, on famine relief work. He used to visit the Moorheads at Annagh-ma-Kerrig. He fell in love with Miss Martha Moorhead, they were married and, in the fullness of time, her home became his home and is now mine.

My father, Dr. Thomas Guthrie came from a long line of Scottish Presbyterian ministers. Far back we have a martyr in the family, a Protestant martyr burnt alive at Saint Andrews by order of Cardinal Beaton. My father's mother was the daughter of Sir John Kirk, a linen manufacturer, who for many years represented South Armagh in the British Parliament. Thus my two grandmothers were raised within thirty miles of one another in the same part of the Ulster border country; but, so far as is known, the two never met. By the time my parents were married, Martha Power was dead and Hannah Guthrie was destined to live for only a few months.

All this family history is to show that my antecedents are Irish—but predominantly Scots-Irish, Ulster-Irish.

I have lived too much abroad to feel vehemently nationalist. And indeed I think vehement nationalism, although political circumstances sometimes make it inevitable, is a disruptive and usually self-indulgent and vainglorious sentiment. I do, however, feel an intense attachment to the region where so many of my kindred have lived and died. One of my dearest hopes is that somehow—not of course spectacularly or publicly, but in a small way, just among the neighbors—my life may be so lived as to promote friendship and mutual tolerance between the two races and the two faiths, which for three hundred years have uneasily and with mutual suspicion co-existed here.

But I'm getting away from the facts.

I am almost six foot five and weigh over two hundred pounds. Six foot five is very tall—almost in the Freak Department—and I have found it quite a cross to bear. If you are six foot five you can't avoid being conspicuous. Now who doesn't want to be conspicuous for riding a rank outsider to victory in the Grand National; for shooting the winning goal at the eleventh hour; for singing La Tosca better than Tebaldi; for being elected Beauty Queen of Inchicore and beating the pants off Miss Portadown, Miss Skegness and that blonde beast Fräulein Düsseldorf. But to be conspicuous just because you're a head taller than all others present—who wants that?

At seventeen to have laughably outgrown your strength as well as your clothes, and to stand there all ankles and wrists with a child's head on top of a beanpole, while aunts say, "My! That boy's grown! What size in shoes do you take *now* dear?" while uncles look at one dubiously and say, "He might make a goalkeeper, if he wasn't such a duffer." At dances to be the most conspicuous, but certainly not the most admired figure on the floor, as you lug round some petite piece, to encircle whose waist you must bend like a hairpin. To be automatically resented by all the plump little would-be Napoleons. To be asked by rude boys if there is snow on top, that is nothing. But, if you're very tall, it's not just rude boys who feel entitled to pass remarks. Perfect strangers in pubs are always coming up and saying, "Me and my friends are just having a bet. Just how tall *are* you?" Women to whom one has just been introduced think that it breaks the ice if they scream, "*Goodness*, you're tall!"

How would they like it if I broke the ice first, by screaming "Goodness, what thick ankles!" or "Goodness what a bust!"

In my case, the cake was taken by a female doctor at a party in Dublin. She caught sign of me, a perfect stranger, across the room, and, in the tones of a macaw, screamed: "Pituitary! Over-development of the pituitary gland!" A silence fell upon the crowded room. Can you wonder? Over-development of the glands! Everyone eyed me as the Macaw backed me against the wall. "My brother was that way," she screamed, gripping my cranium with yellow, scaly claws, "only *his* face was even longer. At the post-mortem they found that the brain was no larger than an egg. Oh look, will you look, he's blushing. No need to blush, dear, it's not your fault."

It was largely to escape from my extremely unwelcome conspicuousness that I wanted to be an actor.

Perhaps this sounds paradoxical. If you don't want to be conspicuous, why get up onto a stage? Well, I don't know: after nearly forty years of it, I've had plenty of time to wonder why people take up the theatre as a profession. Some, it is perfectly true, want to show off, but it is my belief that these are a minority. Far more people go on the stage as a hiding-place, as an escape from the real world, which they find unsatisfactory and feel powerless to change, into a world of make-believe where they can be someone else, an assumed character over whose nature and environment they have some control.

If you think of it, there are many fields where the rank exhibitionist can have far greater scope than in the theatre—in sport, for example. Prominent football players, golfers, pugilists, jockeys command, I would say, a wider and more heartfelt public admiration than any actor.

Of course there's the phenomenon of the stage, film or television "personality." To be a "personality" in this sense you don't have to assume a character in the way that an actor does if he plays Hamlet. You probably make up your own dialogue and what you do off-stage is at least as important as what you do in front of the public. The good opinion of connoisseurs matters less than a prominent position in the gossip column. Nevertheless it requires some degree of art to select and present certain aspects of *yourself*. And you do have to master some of the techniques of acting. You must learn, for instance how to control an audience—to feel its pulse, so to speak—to know when it must be stimulated and when relaxed, when to go faster or slower, when to speak louder and when more quietly. You discover that the way to gain attention is not to speak loudly and insistently. A little of that goes a very long way. In a minute you'll be nagging and nobody wants to be nagged. The way to ensure attention from an audience—be it an audience of a thousand, or two or three gathered together—is to make people believe that you're just going to say something which they don't want to miss. Now the thing which nobody wants to miss is a secret.

Suggest that a cat is about to come out of a bag; suggest, if you can, a certain spiciness; suggest that this particular secret is most certainly not for the children and probably it might be better if Auntie Kathleen didn't hear it either. *Expectation* is the great thing. It really doesn't matter if, when it eventually comes, the anticipated remark is rather dull. If its expectation has been sufficiently aroused, an audience really doesn't notice *what* you say.

This is why a good comedian can get away with such really murderous jokes; the audience has been prepared, conditioned. It's why a good master of ceremonies can make some simply terrible quiz game seem quite amusing. Some skill, some artifice is required.

Let's put it this way: you can be a personality if you've got enough charm or wit or good looks; but to continue to be a personality you've got to do a certain amount of intelligent, hard work.

Where were we? Oh, yes, about the stage being not so much a stamping-ground for exhibitionists as a hide-out for the maladjusted.

Now I wouldn't want you to think that I'd gone on the stage simply and solely because I was badly adjusted to being so tall. There was a better reason than that. I was stage-struck.

A stage-struck youth. Oh dear, how soppy it sounds!

But honestly is it any worse than being "struck" on anything else? Motorcycling or birdwatching or religion. Some activities are more serious and important than others. But some young people are more serious and important than others. It's the nature of young people to be "struck" on things—at least of ardent young people. And it seems to me to be far worse to lack ardor than to be rather soppily "struck" on this or that. Youth and soppiness are rather easily curable diseases. It's age and the disillusion of long experience which are incurable. Soppiness can be got over like measles—gradually the spots disappear and the temperature returns to normal—but if you are fortunate, what begins as a soppy "crush" gradually develops into a lifelong enthusiasm, tempered by the discrimination and, yes, the disillusion which experience inevitably brings.

Unless a person was wildly stage-struck in youth, and unless that youthful enthusiasm has been strengthened, not weakened by the years, I can think of no adequate reason why he should continue to swell the ranks of so overcrowded, so chancy and so exhausting a profession as the stage.

Talent? I don't think I quite know what talent is. There are certainly masses of people with some ability to act. Out of every hundred people I would guess that at least ten have a considerable aptitude for mimicry, for characterization, for telling a story. But only the tiniest minority of these people ever really cultivate their talent, ever really bother to analyze how they achieve their results, ever really work at voice production, at making their bodies more expressive, ever work to widen and deepen their imaginative and intellectual backgrounds, ever apply themselves to the administrative as well as the technical problems of how to make their talent available and useful. Talent is nothing unless it bears fruit. This it can do only if cultivated and fertilized by unremitting, slogging work—physical, mental, and moral.

Of course, opportunity is important. In many ways it helps if, for instance, you are in a position to pay for tuition, to meet people socially who are useful and important, to travel and see what fellow-professionals are doing in other places. But the longer I live the more am I convinced that those who are going to succeed make their own opportunities. If, for example, an actor wants to learn to speak well, it is not necessary, nor even necessarily advantageous, to come from a home, or have been at schools where good speech was cultivated. Dame Edith Evans, the greatest exponent in our day of high comedy, whose speaking is the most elaborate exercise in aristocratic rococo, began life as a milliner's apprentice. Her family lived in a working-class district in south London; and, to the end of his days, her old father spoke in an accent which could hardly have been less ducal. But it was an environment in which a gifted, musical and energetic child could learn—not just book-learning, but learning through the five senses by acquiring, as an artist instinctively does, the impressions which would be useful and relevant to her art. Book-learning, a conventional "good" education, is not necessarily a help to an artist. It tends to inhibit instinct. Learned people are seldom creative, and creative people are seldom learned.

Poverty, I believe, is less of a handicap to a young artist than affluence. Wealthy youngsters rarely do well in the arts. They have to learn, often through bitter disappointment, that their economic privilege does not make them any more clever, beautiful, energetic or imaginative than less moneyed competitors. What wealth does is to offer a number of distracting choices and temptations which bewilder the mind, enfeeble the will, and bedevil the concentration. I have seen more young lives shipwrecked by too many opportunities than by too few.

My being stage-struck was not, I like to hope, entirely a matter of chance or youthful caprice. I may have inherited some inclination toward the theatre. My mother's grandfather, Tyrone Power, was the leading exponent of Irish comedy in his day. He was drowned returning from America in 1840. My father's grandfather was, at about the same time, a leading exponent of the Presbyterian faith in Scotland. Of course, thumping the pulpit cushions is but a hair's breadth from treading the boards. And of the two great-grandparents, Doctor Guthrie, the minister, with his leonine head, his rich ringing voice, his immense renown as an orator and raconteur, was far the more theatrical figure of the two.

The generation after these two was not particularly histrionic. Doctor Guthrie's son, my grandfather, was also a minister, but an inconspicuous one. My mother's father, the actor's son, bore his father's name, Tyrone Power, but did not follow in his professional footsteps. He was a soldier and I think that my mother, who admired him immensely, would have liked me to have been the same. My father would have liked me to be a surgeon, like himself. But no pressure was brought to bear, except that I was sent to a very military, very English and, to me, very uncongenial school, called Wellington, after the Iron Duke.

From there, still undecided about my future, I won a scholarship to Oxford. This gave me a year or two in which, without undue expense to the family, I could decide at what to aim. With a good degree in history and philosophy the possibilities would not be too bad. It was during the Oxford years that I became stage-struck. I did quite a lot of amateur acting. I played a lot of tennis and hockey. I made a number of friends. It was all very pleasant and, in all sorts of ways, very developing. I don't regard the three years as having been misspent; but, at the end of them, I took a most inglorious degree.

It was the end of a pleasant chapter. I still had no sensible idea about my own future, but vaguely optimistic and complacent ideas were suddenly seen to be quite unfounded. I examined the cards in my hand and the very highest I could see was the nine of clubs.

Out of the blue came a letter from James B. Fagan. He had directed one of the amateur plays in which I had acted. He was a professional director of some standing. He was an Irishman from Belfast, he was offering parts to one or two youngsters whom he believed to have promise. Would I like to join the company?

Would I like! By return mail he received my enthusiastic and definite acceptance. I then showed his letter to my father and asked his advice. I guess my father knew that this was rather a formality. But perhaps sons only *think* that their fathers read them like an open book. Anyway, he was nice about it and agreed that, since my prospects were otherwise a total blank, I was in no position to refuse work of any kind—even acting.

The opening play was to be *Heartbreak House* by Bernard Shaw. My part was to be Captain Shotover, the very showy and effective leading role. The salary would be five pounds a week. In those days—1923—you could live easily on five pounds; without a family to support you could even save a little. And anyway, I reflected, my salary won't always be five pounds; after all, one is making a splendid beginning with a leading part. No need to worry because the money—just at present—is rather low.

Came the first rehearsal. I had had all summer to learn my part and was word-perfect. The other, seasoned and professional, actors were far from perfect; they had been grinding away, poor things, on tour and at the Old Vic and so on. They stumbled and muttered and peered at their scripts through spectacles. Never mind; very likely they would improve. I shouted and ranted and carried on, waving my arms and making the sudden, thrilling pauses which had been so effective in amateur dramatics. At lunchtime Mr. Fagan beckoned to me. He took me gently by the arm and walked me up and down the basement corridor of the church hall where we were rehearsing. I can still see the three trash cans and a door marked *Mr. Fothergil Strictly Private.*

It had all been a great mistake, Mr. Fagan was saying, his mistake, not mine. I had talent, he was sure, of sorts; but I wasn't nearly experienced or mature enough for such a large part. "You're rather young, aren't you, for your age. How old are you? Nineteen?" Twenty-three, I had to confess, aware of development abnormally, absurdly retarded. "Ah well," he said kindly, "you've plenty of time ahead."

He also said I might leave then and there, not even come back after lunch. Or, if I liked, I could stay on and make myself as useful as so inept a creature could be. There would be floors to sweep, hampers to pack, lavatories to clean.

Of course I stayed. And I never regretted the decision.

I cleaned the lavs with a will, but in more artistic departments I wasn't much use to the company. I could, if anybody wanted, make quite a striking impression as a ferocious, drunken beggar or a mad, blind Emperor of ninety. But as a presentable, attractive, useful actor, I clearly had no future whatsoever. Luckily I was no less aware of this than everyone else; and realized that my interest lay in direction rather than in acting.

I cannot be sufficiently grateful to Mr. Fagan. He gave me my chance. He was frank, kind and sensible when I turned out to be inadequate; and then, after the debacle, supported me by his goodwill and indication that he believed that, sometime and in some inexplicable way, a spark of talent might appear.

That's the best thing, I think, that older people can do for beginners in the same profession: bolster up their self-confidence, show that they believe you may eventually have something to offer.

And now, after almost forty years, I can't help wondering what have I to offer?

I've been almost continuously busy.

I've been able to keep financially solvent.

I've had the chance to travel all over the world, not just as a tourist, but in the course of professional duty.

I've been privileged to serve the Old Vic over a long period, first, as far back as 1933, as director of the Shakespeare company, then, as the Director of the Old Vic and Sadler's Wells, as successor to the great Lilian Baylis, and finally as a member of the Board of Governors.

I was the first artistic director of the Shakespeare Festival at Stratford, Ontario—a pioneer project on this continent, with which I am very proud to have been connected. I have assisted with the establishment of a classical repertory company in a handsome new theatre in Minneapolis.

Oh, I've enjoyed it all very much indeed, especially the companionship in which all kinds of the oddest people mingle and find common ground in their enthusiasm for their job.

But what has it all been in aid of? What cause has been served? When I was younger I used to think that, if I worked very earnestly and hard, and if I only directed plays which I believed to be "good" plays, that then my work might have an uplifting, an ennobling effect upon the human race. I don't quite know when I gave up that belief, but it was quite a good many years ago.

To begin with, I don't know what constitutes a "good"

play; and, to go on, I think it's impudence to set about uplifting and ennobling your fellow-citizens. It implies that you know not only what is good for you, but also what is good for them. This doesn't mean that I think the theatre is no more than a place of frivolous entertainment. It can be that, of course, and very often is. But it can be far, far more. It can be the means of arousing the most profound reflections, the most vivid passions, the most serene joys. But who knows just how and when and why? I most certainly don't.

A great play, dully performed, can be a great bore. A trifle, greatly performed, can be a tremendous experience. What may seem a great experience to me may seem to you just a waste of time and energy. I should think a person who could sit unmoved and unimpressed through a half-decent performance of *Oedipus Rex* must be either a boor or a half-wit. But honestly, who is to say what constitutes a half-decent performance?

I feel that after forty years I have achieved some mastery in a limited repertory of the tricks of the trade, some knowledge of my own limitations, technical and spiritual, and a certainty that I do not know very well what is good, and not at all what will be popular. I might have lived a more useful life as a soldier, or as the doctor my father would have liked me to be, as a farmer, a schoolmaster, in business, in the church or in a bank. Who knows? But it's too late now to change, even if I wanted to.

I don't want to. I think the best I can do now is to keep what assets I have in circulation, and I think my principal asset is experience, just the simple fact that I've been at it for a long while. After you pass sixty you begin to feel just a little less energy and perhaps a little less enthusiasm than you used to—at all events a different sort of enthusiasm. Also, many of your ideas are bound to seem to young people rather old-fashioned. That's not important, unless you yourself are silly enough to think so. I don't think any such thing. I believe that I can still be useful in projects which do not depend upon being up-to-date, fashionable, topical. I *know* that there are more important qualities, of which sound professional workmanship is one.

Well there! I guess I haven't exactly painted a self-portrait. I've tried rather to imply it, by talking about things which are an important part, not just of what I do, but what I am.

2. THEATRE AS RITUAL

THIS IS GOING TO BE about religion, I am not a theological scholar, nor equipped in any way to speak with authority. To serve the theatre is my profession; it is my belief that, in trying to serve the theatre faithfully, I am offering some sort of service to God.

What manner of God?

If you believe that every word of the Bible is literally, factually true then I think that you ought to skip this piece. What I'm going to say will probably make you very angry; and, though I shall not say anything deliberately irreverent or impious, you, with your beliefs, may very well think so.

The Athenian civilization has never been surpassed in the history of mankind, and to it, in many respects, our own civilization is inferior. In the course of nearly two thousand five hundred years some of this civilization has disappeared, but in the fields of philosophy, drama, sculpture and architecture, Athens makes our contemporary efforts seem puny. In politics Athens has been the model for subsequent democracies. It is true that Athenian democracy did not last for very long and collapsed under the stress of war with Sparta, which was not democratically organized.

But what remains of Sparta now? Even its site is barely identifiable. Sparta left no works of art or literature, no system of laws; even its gymnastic training, upon which the efficiency of its marvelously efficient soldiers was built, even this remains as no more than a vague legend in Athenian history. Whereas Athens has exercised an incalculably important influence upon the whole of Western civilization.

Now what of the religion of the Athenians?

What did the people who created such marvelous political and philosophic systems, such marvelous works of art—what did these people worship?

Even in the sophisticated days of Athenian supremacy—in the fifth century B.C.—the official religion still asserted the existence of the Homeric deities. There was Zeus, the King and Father of all Gods, perhaps more familiar to us by his Roman name, Jupiter; there was Hera, the sister-wife of Zeus, and a multitude of other gods, who were thought of as the family of Zeus and Hera. Their life was a tumult of passion and was imagined—rather vaguely—to take place on Mount Olympus—a mountain as real as Mount Sinai. The Olympian deities were a survival into a sophisticated era of far more primitive conceptions; and I believe that the attitude toward them of sophisticated fifth century Athenians may have been analogous with that of sophisticated people of our own generation toward the violent, jealous, capricious deity, who dominates the earlier books of the Old Testament.

Do most of us believe that the world was made by God in six days? I regard this as a primitive myth, which states in very splendid and majestic simplicity the belief that our material setting owes its existence to some great power and is part of a plan, which we do not understand, but which we timidly hope and devoutly believe to be benevolent. Our imagination, no different in this from that of children or very primitive people, can only conceive the begetter of a plan and the source of benevolence in the image of our own begetter and the principal source of benevolence in our own experience—a Father. We say that God the Father created us in His image. But I think this means no more than that we create Him in ours.

Likewise, do we believe that Moses went up the side of Mount Sinai—no less real than Mount Olympus—and returned bearing two tables of stone, upon which were engraved the Ten Commandments? Surely this is a poetic statement of the fact that Moses codified ten very practical rules for conducting the life of a community. The mountain, a high place, symbolizes the notion that God dwells above us, in a more exalted station. The same idea is implicit in Olympus, or, for that matter, Heaven, the sky. The tables being of stone symbolize the strength and indestructibility of the commandments. It is possible that Moses caused them to be engraved upon tables of stone; but one can hardly credit that even Moses could have scrambled down the side of a precipitous mountain, carrying two great stone tablets.

When Aeschylus wrote his tragedy of *Prometheus Bound* I think it is very clear that he did not believe that Prometheus had ever, in strict fact, been chained by order of Zeus to a rock. The drama makes it very clear that the poet's attitude to Zeus was not one of unquestioning reverence. The audience is encouraged to feel that, in punishing Prometheus, the Father of the Gods is being not only cruel but petty and capricious. And the criticism implied is not irreverent because it is inspired by such a deeply considered and passionate humanism.

Likewise, in *Oedipus,* Sophocles follows the facts of legend in all its primitive violence and simplicity. But his comment is sophisticated. He is dealing with one of the perennial puzzles in man's relation to God: why, through no apparent fault of their own, are certain men singled out for disaster? In Hebrew mythology the same theme occupies the Book of Job. Sophocles attempts no direct or easy answer to the paradox. The tone of the tragedy, I would say, is extremely reverent, inasmuch as, though an evident injustice on the part of God to Man is implied, it is made clear that the injustice only appears so from a human standpoint. Again and again the symbols of sight and blindness, light and dark, are invoked, and the suggestion underlying the whole tragedy I take to be that we, with our limited vision, by the feeble light of human intelligence, are unable to discern our origin and must proceed blindly toward our darkly incomprehensible destiny.

What, you may ask, has all this to do with the theatre? We are coming there, albeit by a roundabout route.

It is my belief that we, like the Athenians, have a sneaking belief in many gods. The first commandment on Moses' tablets was, you may recall, "I am the Lord thy God . . . thou shalt have no other gods before me." A strict, categorical insistence on Monotheism. One God, only one. Thereafter, those who accepted Jehovah had to forego all other deities, and the early books of the Old Testament are largely filled with the frightful things which happened to those who disobeyed.

Are we, likewise, guilty of disobedience in this matter? Do we, in fact, worship one God, and only one?

With what the devout believe to be Divine Authority, we accept the illogical and, to me, unintelligible doctrine of a Holy Trinity—three in one and one in three. Is this one God? Or is it three?

Further, while we pretend that we do not worship them, we pay to certain other conceptions a reverence which I find myself unable to distinguish from worship. We pray—or rather those of Roman Catholic faith do so—to the Blessed Virgin Mary, to "intercede" for us with the Almighty Father. Of course, if we believe in a Father-God it is only natural, being made the way we are, to believe in a Mother-God as well. But surely to do so considerably stretches the meaning of the first commandment. Then there are all the lesser, but still sacred, beings to whom we intermittently pray—Saint Anthony, for instance, who was forever "finding" my Cousin Kathleen's needlecase.

I am aware that the Roman Catholic church makes three theoretic distinctions between the worship due to Almighty God, that due to the Blessed Virgin, and that due to the saints; and I think I can see that for very sophistical devotees the distinction may have some meaning other than intellectual. But I am convinced that for the vast majority, as for me, the distinction is solely a matter of terminology.

But even if we belong to a more northern and Protestant faith, which pays far less attention to sanctified and beatified beings, even then we offer to certain ideas a reverence which may, I suppose, be distinguishable from worship—but only just. Many of us offer such reverence to our mothers, our fathers, to wife, husband or child. You may say that what is offered is not worship but love. Is there a difference? Is it entirely inaccurate when we say of Smith that he "worships" Mrs. Smith, while she, in turn "idolizes" Smith Junior?

I know, and so do you, a great many people who worship Money, or Success, or Celebrity; and a great many more who worship Conformity and Respectability. They do not perhaps actually kneel down and address petitions to these gods, but they most certainly do make sacrifices to them—often of their nearest and dearest. Don't you know children who have been sacrificed, literally sacrificed, and by adoring parents with the best of intentions, on the altars of respectability and conformity? And don't you know people who offer thanks to such deities? "Thank God, dear, that Daddy's always been such a careful, steady man." What god is being thanked in that speech? The deity who flooded the earth and drowned all its inhabitants, except the Ark party? the furious tribal deity who bade Elijah slaughter the priests of Baal at the Brook Kishon? Was that steady and careful? Or Jesus, who bade us consider the lilies of the fields and take no thought for the morrow? Was that steady and careful?

No. When ladies are thankful that Daddy's always been a steady, careful man, they are thankful to deities of a comparatively humble rank—to Gods of Thrift, Caution, Respectability, as well as to the great gods of Love and Unselfishness. When men say "Thank God your Mother—unlike Mrs. Jones, who eloped with a gasfitter—thank God your mother is a *good* woman!" they are worshipping the Goddess of Chastity, in the Olympian Pantheon a close relation of the Goddess of Love, oddly enough.

Let me repeat: I do not think that we consciously and literally believe, any more than did Sophocles or Aeschylus, in all these minor deities—gods of chastity, respectability, money and so on. But they *influence* us. Can any of us say, whatever his conscious religious beliefs, that he is quite uninfluenced by a

primitive notion of luck? Tens of thousands of churchgoers are
a little bit worried if they break a looking-glass; professors of
Philosophy throw spilt salt over their sophisticated shoulders;
I have myself beheld an Archbishop spit at a magpie.

Whether we like it or no, we are children of the past. We
cannot by saying, "I believe in one God," and by trying to do
so as hard as ever we can, shake off the primitive and polythe-
istic beliefs which we have inherited together with our physical
structure. By trying very hard, we can become less superstitious;
we can reduce superstitious idolatry from a creed to the
status of something of which we are a little ashamed, like fear
of the dark, a weakness to be smiled at but nevertheless acknowledged.

Now perhaps it was a little naïve of the Greeks to imagine
that great quarrelsome brood on Mount Olympus as a family
—a Father and Mother and then a tribe of exceedingly varied
relations, connected by what, in human terms, we should have
to consider odd goings-on. But, in fact, does not this idea symbolize an important truth: namely, that all departments of existence are quite closely, and often unexpectedly, related? That
the God of Battles is, in fact, closely connected with chivalry
and mercy, as well as butchery; that the God of Money encourages the daring of adventure, as well as the caution of
thrift? And this, surely, throws a valuable light upon what is
often regarded as a great paradox in the relation of God to man:
namely, the existence of Evil.

Why does an all-wise, all-powerful God tolerate the existence of sin and disease? I do not think it is possible to deny
that Evil, as well as Good, exists in the world. But does not the
Greek idea of many and closely-related deities help us to understand that Evil and Good are not, in fact, different ideas,
but the same idea viewed from two different standpoints, or
considered in two different contexts? "One man's meat is another man's poison." What seems darkness when one has just
come out of a bright light is gradually seen not to be darkness

at all. Dark and light are not in fact opposites, but different degrees of visibility, as it were, opposite poles of the same axis. Likewise, heat and cold are poles of one axis: what seems cold in one context is revealed as hot in another. So with sorrow and joy. And so with good and evil.

God and Satan are personifications of Good and Evil; and God in one context becomes Satan in another. Thus only, it seems to me, is it possible to believe in one God. Otherwise we have to accept the paradox of an all-powerful God who is powerless to prevent the frequent and disastrous triumph of Evil or Satan—an all-wise God who cannot prevail over folly, an omnipresent God who is absent in the event of evil.

Now let us apply all this to the theatre.

Every action, every thought even, however apparently unimportant, has a cause and an effect. In a justly celebrated passage of *War and Peace* Tolstoi shows how the apparently trivial movement of some little birds in a bush was the immediate cause of the Battle of Borodino, and the beginning of the disastrous end of Napoleon's Russian campaign. Even a tiny trifle is part of the gigantic, infinitely elaborate, chain of cause and effect. Causes apparently trivial are the results of earlier causes, which are not trivial at all. The birds of Borodino were driven by forces of elemental power. They were fidgeting about in their bush because they were cold, or were hungry, or because it was their mating season.

Comparatively speaking, theatrical activity is trivial. I do not want to seem falsely humble; it is no more trivial than most human activity. To have written *Hamlet*, for instance, is no trifle. To be part of a half-decent performance of *Hamlet* is not a trivial way of earning money. But, for the most part, our everyday life in the theatre is trivial enough. Yet each one of us is, like the birds of Borodino, part of The Plan.

But I think the theatre can be related to God in a more precise and a more conscious way: as a religious ritual.

Let me expand this idea.

Like all the rest of nature, we are creatures of habit. We like to find what we believe to be a good way of doing something and then to go on doing it, as nearly as possible, in the same way. Our very thoughts fall into habitual patterns. But the ritual nature of habit is more clearly seen in action than in thought. Let me give an instance and excuse its being a homely one: from a very, very early age humans teach their young a ritual of hygiene. At regular intervals a baby is set upon a pot and encouraged to do what has to be done. The aim is to create habit, and in the vast majority of cases this aim is so successfully achieved that neither in body, nor in mind, are we comfortable unless the ritual has been performed at the appointed time and in the accustomed manner.

It is the same with every one of our habitual activities; and, without being too fanciful, I think we can see all our regular routines as being, not merely a concession to our own conservatism, but also an offering on our part to some aspect of the Almighty. Just as the commuter in train or bus is performing a ritual act in honor of Industry, Punctuality, or some similar aspect of God, so the housewife, with her cooking things, vacuum, needle and thread is equipped for sacrifice to the greater glory of the Household Gods.

The natural desire is to do all these daily chores as nearly as possible in the same way, in the same order and at the same time. Occasionally, however, just for the sake of a change, we will vary our routine. The commuter will walk to the station by Linden Gardens instead of Chestnut Avenue; the housewife will do the laundry on *Tuesday*. But the change is a conscious and deliberate act; it is not a forsaking of ritual, it is merely the substitution of the Benedicite for the Te Deum.

None of these everyday routines, however, is quite consciously a ritual. In the theatre, on the other hand, the ritual nature of proceedings is far more conscious.

We discussed Athens in the beginning, because there the theatre was probably a more serious part of the life of the community than it has ever been at any other time or in any other place; and also because the Athenian theatre, although by the time of its finest flowering it had moved far from its primitive religious origins, was still nominally a religious rite. The annual Athenian dramatic festival was conducted in honor of Dionysus, the God of the Vine. It was a spring festival, concerned with the return of life to the earth after the decay of autumn and the sleep, or death, of winter.

Christian culture has taken over many of the ideas underlying Dionysiac and other more primitive rites of spring. We have purified them, or it could equally be said, emasculated them, by the elimination of much grossness and sexuality. In the Christian festival of spring—Easter—the resurgence of natural forces after the winter is no longer the focus of the rites. It is merely symbolic of the Saviour's resurrection after death. In Christian terms the resurrection gives meaning to all the natural phenomena, including the joy we feel with the return of warmth and fertility to the earth.

In classical Athens the Dionysiac rites, also, had become a great deal more sophisticated and idealized than they had been in more primitive times. It is reasonable to suppose that primitive man, feeling the joy of spring, gave spontaneous expression to his feeling in song and dance and in sexual abandon. But when the same natural phenomena occurred year after year and were celebrated by the same songs, the same dances, they ceased to be spontaneous and gradually hardened into ritual. As spring was perceived to be a regularly recurrent phenomenon, ideas began to be formulated about its origin and purpose. Primitive man, like ourselves, began to believe that he was part of A Plan. The rites of spring began to be not merely stylized expressions of joy, but also of thankfulness, and—a further sophistication—man began to feel, along with gratitude for present mercies, an anxiety that such mercies should continue, that seed-time would be followed by harvest. Ideas of gratitude were mingled with ideas of propitiation— thank you and please.

It is not known precisely how these rites developed, nor precisely what they were. But by comparison with what is known of primitive communities observable in our own day, we may assume that sacrifices were offered to the gods and that the most important rites would have centered upon human sacrifice. Gradually, as man became more sophisticated, the idea of human sacrifice became repellant. In place of humans, animals were offered. The story of the Lord substituting a ram in place of the beloved son whom Abraham was about to offer in sacrifice is perhaps a legendary expression of our growing horror of human sacrifice. Gradually again, the slaughter not only of human beings but of beasts began to offend the taste and the conscience of society. Instead of an actual sacrifice, the offering took symbolic form. A *story* of sacrifice was enacted in honor of the God: a tragedy.

We know that the first actors of tragedy in Athens were priests. They ritually re-enacted the death and resurrection of Dionysus. Note, please, the analogy with our Christian ritual. Christ was sacrificed for us—a human sacrifice—and in the ritual of Holy Communion the priest recapitulates in words certain facts of the passion, or sacrifice, and these words are precisely accompanied by ritual mime, which symbolically commemorates the breaking of Christ's body and the shedding of his blood. In Athens, by the time *Oedipus* was produced, priests had given place to professional actors and the Festival of Drama, while still formally presented in honor of Dionysus, had become considerably secularized. The god principally concerned with Oedipus is not Dionysus, the wine god, but Apollo; and the drama is far from being a simple statement of devotion. It is the product of an extremely skeptical mind; and anyone who has seen it and seriously pondered its meaning can hardly fail to be faced with three or four faith-shaking theological posers.

I hope that I have suggested points in common between Holy Communion and Greek tragedy, no more, perhaps, than that both are commemorations of the passion, or agony, of great personages, brought about by violent and mistaken, but by no means always ill-intentioned, acts.

I hope now to establish a similar connection between Shakespearean and modern tragedy.

Let us take *Macbeth* as an instance. Naturally, like any other great work of art, *Macbeth* offers many possible interpretations. But two themes are inescapably dominant and must be an important part of any and every interpretation: ambition and murder. The murder, moreover, is of a particular kind. Duncan is an old man; he is of an age to be Macbeth's father. He is also Macbeth's King, and a king is a kind of father. The regicide is a sort of father-murder. In this respect the tragedy of King Macbeth bears a striking resemblance to that of King Oedipus. There are further resemblances: both the doomed protagonists were men of very exceptional courage, intelligence and sensibility; both were fatally guided by what they believed to be supernatural promptings.

The analogy cannot be pursued too far. Shakespeare's technical methods and his cast of mind were very different from those of Sophocles. But I hope you will agree that the two tragedies have striking similarities. It is not hard to find similar analogies, which link all great tragedies and show them to be concerned with the passion, or suffering of a great personage. I suggest that the nature of tragedy has not changed. Macbeth, Hamlet, Phaedra, Faust, Becket, even Willy Loman in *Death of a Salesman,* are all, like the protagonists of Greek tragedy, victims at a ceremony of sacrifice, where, though the victim is not physically carved up, his passion is ritually commemorated, relived in word and deed.

Again may I draw your attention to the analogy with the Christian ritual of Holy Communion. Just as in Holy Communion, just as in *Oedipus,* so in *Macbeth* is the ritual concerned with the re-enactment of a passion or sacrifice. King Macbeth, like King Oedipus, and like Jesus of Nazareth, King of the Jews, is the victim of forces which bring him to his destruction; and by participating in the ritual, the audience, or congregation, goes with the victim along a Via Dolorosa which leads either to Golgotha, to Kithairon or to Dunsinane. The actor, who impersonates Macbeth, is the priest whose duty it is, with a liturgy of words and gesture, to commemorate the sacrifice of a crowned king. He is directly connected by historical sequence with his forerunners, who, as priests at the altar, shed the blood of human sacrifice. The bloodshed now is symbolical, imaginary; but the ritual is still concerned with sacrifice.

The principal difference between Shakespearean, or indeed modern, tragedy, and that of classical Athens is concerned, not with the kind of drama, but the purpose of its presentation.

As we have seen, the purpose of the Athenian Festival of Drama was religious. For many centuries after the fall of Athens, drama still continued to be the servant of religion. Right up until the Reformation, English drama occupied itself with religious subjects, was presented with the approval, and usually under the auspices, of the church on the occasions of the great religious festivals—Christmas, Easter, Corpus Christi, and so on. The Reformation effected a divorce between the two. Henceforth drama became a wholly, and often a rather defiantly, secular activity. The Reformed Church disapproved of playacting. It was considered at best frivolous, and often licentious as well. Shortly after Shakespeare's death (1616) public theatrical performances were, in England, forbidden by law (1642), and were not legally permitted until the Restoration of the monarchy in 1660.

Now I suppose one can never postulate a single purpose in connection with any activity. Motives are always mixed. In such an activity as play-production, where a number of people are involved, with a number of different axes to grind, and where the activity is sustained over quite long periods of time, it is quite impossible to assign a single purpose. But I think it would be reasonable to say that the medieval theatre was dominated, just like the Greek, by a religious intention. There were naturally other purposes: human vanity, for instance would have been involved, as in any other form of self-expression. But the over-all intention was to celebrate an ecclesiastical occasion and, by enacting scriptural incidents, to make them a more vivid part of ordinary people's consciousness.

After the Reformation the consciously religious purpose disappeared, and artistic intention became altogether more confused. A new and dominant motive appeared: commercial profit.

We simply do not know how much the commercial motive influenced Shakespeare. We do know that William Shakespeare of Stratford-upon-Avon died in very comfortable circumstances. But if Shakespeare considered—as from the title we have a right to conclude—that *As You Like It* was really what the public liked, then it is hard to believe that he would have written *Measure for Measure,* say, or *King Lear,* or *Coriolanus* under the influence of the profit motive. It seems much more credible that he chose his themes because they interested him, because he had something which he felt impelled to express—the dominant motive of most creative writing.

But, though the creative artists of the theatre may be concerned with self-expression, more and more the theatre has, since the Reformation, been dominated not by artists but by men of business. And the dominant motive of business is financial profit.

Again, we must say dominant. It is not the sole motive. Nor are the theatre's men of business just merchants and nothing more. Shakespeare, for instance, was a man of business, a shareholder and director of theatrical companies, a speculator in theatrical real estate. So have been many of the theatre's greatest artists. It is an absurd fallacy to think that artists are all unpractical, childlike things, with no notion at all of how many beans make five. It is equally absurd to think that all men of business are illiterate, greedy philistines.

By and large, however, the *dominant* purpose of theatrical management is success, and the only objective way to measure success is in terms of receipts at the box-office. "Artistic success" is a matter, not of fact, but of entirely subjective opinion.

Now back to the main line of the argument: the theatre and God. How does our modern, secular theatre, whose creators are dominated by the need for self-expression, and whose organizers and distributors by the need for a success solely measurable in terms of cash—how does such a theatre relate itself to God?

If God is all-knowing, all-powerful, omnipresent and benevolent he must accept responsibility for an activity which is secular, as well as for religious activities. There must, in short, be a relation. Let us see if this relation is more understandable if, for a moment, we imagine that a single Almighty God is theoretically divisible into a system, or hierarchy, not unlike that of the Olympians. Is this blasphemous? or even impious?

Think of a city—say, London, or Paris, or New York. We conceive of it as a unity; we are most of us sufficiently primitive to personify that unity, to think of Paris, for instance, as a woman. But we know that a great city is an infinitely complicated amalgam of people and things and activities, ideas and institutions. The Parks Board is King, or God, over certain territories; the Education Board has another kingdom; Water Supply, Sewage or Garbage Disposal, Organized Religion, Organized Vice, Hospitals, Public Transport—there are a legion of separately governed, but closely interlocked, kingdoms. We cannot begin to understand, or practically to relate ourselves to the unity, unless we appreciate that, as well as being one, it is manifold.

Take another instance, another kind of city in a way, a human body. Each of us is a separate entity, an individual. But, for practical purposes, we have to break ourselves up, as it were, into many component parts. We should think pretty lowly of a doctor who, on the ground that the human body was a single entity, attempted to cure earache by amputating a foot.

Now consider God, one and—theologically—indivisible. At the same time, poetically and metaphorically, God has always been infinitely divisible: God of Hosts, God of Mercy, God of

Wrath, The Friend of Little Children, of the poor and the oppressed, God the Father, and God the Son, the Holy Ghost, the Dove, the Hound of Heaven, the Voice in the Whirlwind and the Still, Small Voice . . . within a theological unity, infinitely manifold.

Assuming, then, that God is metaphorically divisible, let us see if a theatrical performance cannot be regarded as a ritual performed in honor of certain of God's many aspects, just as the Athenian dramatic festival was offered in honor of the God of the Vine.

Oedipus, though offered as part of the Festival of Dionysus, was really more concerned with man's relation to Apollo, God of Light and Enlightenment. Similarly, *Macbeth,* in our modern theatre, is offered in a temple, dedicated for the most part to moneymaking and frivolity. But neither of these objects is likely to be the purpose of a production of *Macbeth,* which is renowned neither as moneymaker nor laugh-getter. May not the purpose of a performance of *Macbeth* be to reveal a great work of art to the public, to reveal something about the nature of mankind, even the nature of God; also to seek the compassion of the audience for the hero's agony, and its awe at the spectacle of ruined greatness?

Therefore, might not *Macbeth* have been regarded in Athenian theatre as an offering to the God of Light and Enlightenment? Likewise, to the Gods of Justice, Pity and Awe? Therefore may not we, of the Christian and monotheistic tradition, invoke, not several deities, but such aspects of the one Almighty God as are concerned with enlightenment, justice, pity, and awe?

Such aspects of God as these are invoked in the case of tragedy, the theatre's solemn rites. But, thank goodness, the rites of the theatre are not always solemn.

Maybe we are not quite solemn enough. In our commercial system we have too many plays, of which the aim is rather pitifully frivolous. Six out of ten commercial comedies are content to tell a story with no more ambition than to amuse the public by appealing to its sexual appetite, its sense of humor and its vanity. The dominant purpose behind their presentation is rather trivial too: to make money and to gratify personal ambition. Nevertheless such comedies as these are also of a ritual nature. Age-old devices are used in their construction to create tension and then get laughs; the very term "antic," denoting the goings-on of funny men and tumblers, by derivation means antique or old. I suppose the gods, or aspects of Almighty God, in honor of whom these rites are performed, are concerned with mirth, sex, satire, vanity and moneymaking.

A third kind of play may have a fantastic story and its appeal may be chiefly visual or musical. Of this kind are the romances of Shakespeare, or Mozart's *The Magic Flute,* or most ballets. Clearly in Athens entertainments like these would belong to Apollo. But the One God, too, has revealed aspects of Himself which are graciously inclined toward offerings of music, dancing and poetry.

You may think perhaps that it invalidates the argument if theatrical people as a whole are not aware of the hieratic quality of their work. I daresay that some striptease girls are not entirely conscious that they are priestesses in the Temple of Aphrodite. Equally, I daresay, some savages are not aware of the meaning of Rain Dances or War Dances. Yet the rite does not lose all meaning because certain members of the tribe are jumping about for no better reason than that others are jumping about, or even just for fun. All theatrical performances, from *Oedipus* to striptease, are conducted, like war dances, like rain dances, according to age-old formulae. Here and there innovations are made. They seem at the time to be important; the innovations of Ibsen, for instance, seemed so revolutionary no more than seventy years ago that critics screamed with rage and foamed at the mouth. But already Ibsen has been absorbed into the mainstream of dramatic tradition and seems to us, in our particular era, to be far more old-fashioned than Sophocles or Shakespeare. The stream flows on. Effect follows effect and becomes cause and effect. The Great Plan unrolls. And we, from the greatest, most eminent and brilliant genius of the theatre down to the checktaker in the grubbiest little striptease joint, from millennium to millennium, proclaim ourselves part of The Plan, proclaim to its Author our gratitude for mercies past, our hope for mercy to come. Thank you and please.

Let me sum up. The theatre relates itself to God by means of ritual. It does so more consciously than any other activity, except prayer, because, like organized prayer, it is the direct descendant of primitive religious ceremonies.

This, however, does not sanctify the theatre. It does not make it either good or bad. Its rites are related not to human morality but to God. God has no more connection with what we humans like to call moral than with what we like to call immoral. All-knowing, all-powerful, He is in charge of the entire Plan, and the plan includes the frivolous as well as the serious, the evil as well as the good.

3. CLASSICAL THEATRE AND THE ENTERTAINMENT INDUSTRY

THE GREATEST PERIOD in the history of the theatre was, in my opinion, that which produced in Athens the work of Aeschylus, Sophocles, Euripides and Aristophanes. We know that there were other Athenian dramatists whose work has not survived. The lost works may have been as great or greater than any of those surviving. We know that much of the work of the great four has been destroyed, and that too often even the surviving works are incomplete.

It would be foolish to say that any single one of the four is a greater dramatist than Shakespeare, or Molière, even than Ibsen. It would be like saying that chalk is greater than cheese.

I guess one might say that *Oedipus* is the most economically and powerfully constructed play which has even been written. But the character of King Oedipus is not as interestingly or fully revealed as that of Hamlet, Macbeth or Lear; the dialogue is not so witty nor so sharp as that of Molière; the events do not present the great panorama of a human life like *Peer Gynt*. But it is not upon the glory of individual plays that the greatness of the Greek theatre depends. What makes it supreme is the fact that Athens then offered a set-up, a physical and, more important, spiritual environment, which made possible the creation of masterpieces.

Let us consider some of the features of this environment.

In the first place, Athens was not, by modern standards, a large city. Scholars are generally agreed that the number of citizens was no more than two hundred thousand. In addition there was a slave population of about double that number. Furthermore, because of its geographical situation, Athens is, and must always have been, a highly compact city. This is important. It seems to me that Los Angeles, for example, sprawling as it does over an immense area, will have the utmost difficulty in ever achieving any semblance of metropolitan status or culture. Already there exists an immense and very lively university; there are churches, art galleries, libraries, a symphony orchestra, an intermittent but star-spangled opera, all housed at least adequately, some sumptuously. But these temples are islands situated in a vast sea of sun-drenched, peach-fed, pale pink and silver vacuity.

In Athens you can still easily walk to the Parthenon from any part of the city. Classical Athens was even more compact. This gave to Athenian society a homogeneity which no great modern city possesses. London, Paris, New York have all had, and still have, homogeneous groups or cliques. But the oneness of these groups has largely been the result of feeling that they were a small band of brothers in a society which, if not actually hostile, was certainly indifferent to all which they held dear or important.

This is not to say that in Athens there was a perfect social and political unanimity. We know that it was not so. There were strong and frequently violent partisanships and rivalries in politics, in art, and in sport as well. But it seems to me that these were rifts in the surface of a deeply homogeneous society.

Something similar could be seen in mid-Victorian London. There was strong political opposition between the parties of Disraeli and Gladstone, strong social opposition between radical reformers and upholders of the good old ways, strong opposition between high church and low church, between Philistine and Aesthete, "the greenery-yallery, Grosvenor Gallery, foot-in-the-grave young man." But in spite of all this there continued to exist a tightly and very consciously homogeneous upper-class, known as "Society." Society remained solidly bound together by ties of common self-interest far deeper than the superficial divisions which rent it apart. Society managed to maintain an exclusive oligarchy, holding an extraordinary proportion of the country's wealth and power, in spite of divisions within and ever-increasing pressure from without. It was not until 1914–18, when seven out of ten of the heirs to this oligarchy were killed or hopelessly maimed in Flanders, that society began to fall apart, and the power and the glory passed into other hands.

So in Athens, it was not until the long-drawn struggle with Sparta had sapped the energy, exhausted the material resources and destroyed the heirs, that Athenian "Society," hitherto tightly homogeneous in spite of violent differences and rivalries, began to fall apart. It is often said that this homogeneity of Athenian society was achieved because of the use of slaves. By relegating the hardest and dullest work to slaves, Athenian citizens achieved the leisure to develop their civilization, and the fear that the slaves might rebel and destroy them was the strongest tie which held society together. This may be true.

But before we think ourselves superior to the Athenians, let us question whether the so-called Freedom of the Western Democracies is quite so complete as we like to suppose. The hardest and dullest work is no longer done by slaves. But it is done by a proletariat which, though financially often well-rewarded, is still in many ways as under-privileged as the Athenian slave. Furthermore, the measure of political, social and financial freedom which we have achieved has, arguably, been at the expense of our spiritual freedom. Has there ever been an age when an affluent society has been so completely the slave of its own conventions? We are slaves to the fear of doing and saying the wrong thing, slaves to the desire—so strong as to be an absolute need—to wear the right clothes, eat the right meals, send our children to the right schools, have the right vacations, even the right illnesses and finally, the right interment. "Right" in every case meaning as like as possible to everyone else in our particular social group.

It is my view that, except for the fact that we no longer use the term slave to denote those at the bottom of the ladder of privilege, our society is no more free than that of Athens and a great deal less cultivated and homogeneous.

It was this cultivated homogeneous society which enabled the Athenian drama to flourish. The drama was an expression of society's viewpoint—a mixture of religious, political and social traditions gradually formed over many generations. I do not think the gradual nature of this process is sufficiently realized. It is customary to assume that some people just *have* good taste, that they toil not, neither do they spin to acquire it. This simply is not so. Some people have more intelligence and sensitivity than others and therefore learn more quickly and easily. But taste in art, as in food, is something which has to be cultivated. Children's taste is naïve. They like sweet, sweet food and bright colors and pretty, tinkly music. Many people retain childish tastes to the end of their days, but most acquire more sophisticated tastes as part of the whole gradual process of maturity.

A taste for art can only be acquired by exposing yourself to art, by looking at pictures, for instance, until you acquire an instinctive, subconscious feeling for line, texture, color, composition, and so on. Then you begin to ask yourself why El Greco is considered to be a more interesting painter than Rockwell Kent, unquestionably a splendid craftsman, whose work you perhaps used to admire rather more than you do now. By such, or by analogous, steps do you refine your own taste. It takes time and energy.

By such, or by analogous, steps does a community form its taste. Only after several generations have spent time and energy on the process, do results begin to be gradually apparent. Thinking becomes clearer, language becomes at once richer and simpler, legislation more humane. More sophisticated taste expresses itself in dress, in furniture, in architecture. Sophisticated taste is seldom fussy and is apt to rate economy of means higher than expensive elaboration. Let us avoid saying "good" or "bad" taste since, in this case, good and bad are entirely subjective, and also extremely fluid, terms. What you may think is bad may to me seem good; what we both admire this year will probably ten years from now seem dated and dowdy.

The taste of classical Athens had been formed in a relatively short time. The community changed from peasant simplicity to a state of humane sophistication, greater probably than any other community has since achieved, in a matter of a few centuries. France and Britain were far slower in maturing.

In America sophistication is still perhaps a little more apparent than real, because material wealth, on a scale unprecedented in the world's history, has enabled people to buy a great deal of material evidence of a sophistication which they do not really possess. In any midwestern city, for example, there will be several restaurants which boast a French cuisine, sometimes excellent, sometimes strictly bogus, furnished in Louis Quinze style with incredibly luxurious carpets, crystal chandeliers, china, glass and linen of fine quality. But the massive and hairy gentlemen, bursting out of expensive suits, and the ladies, clinking with charm bracelets, slung with mink and diamonds, do not always match their elegant surroundings. The surroundings are not at present an expression of their own taste, which, as their clothes, their voices, gestures, and vocabulary proclaim, is considerably more crude.

What matter? They are learning. Their children will learn more. The wealth is enabling them to assimilate a sophistication in two or three generations, which in Europe probably took ten or twelve.

The point is that the process takes time. It cannot be hurried. No one must feel badly because, at this point, America has not been able to achieve the sophistication of classical Athens, and thence because the American theatre still lags many centuries behind the Athenian theatre of Sophocles, the English theatre of Shakespeare, or the French theatre of Molière. Furthermore, let no one think that the American theatre can buy itself into the big league. It must win its way thither by a gradual process of education through experience, which will inevitably take several generations.

Americans are impatient and disinclined to let things grow slowly. In art, as in horticulture, a forced rapidity of growth may produce a briefly showy florescence. In long terms it gets nowhere.

Now back to Athens.

It is essential to remember that the performances—or at all events the most important performances—were part of the festival of the god Dionysus.

We cannot, I think, underestimate the importance which this religious element gave to the drama in Greece. Contrast it with the position of drama in other epochs. Roman society was essentially philistine. Military and commercial activities were "serious"; art, science and philosophy were merely leisure pursuits, amusements, embellishments. The Roman theatre never expressed, as did the Greek, the deepest belief and aspiration of the audience.

After the fall of the Roman Empire, a professional theatre, so far as we know, ceased to exist. Great noblemen had their own fools and jesters, there were jongleurs, there may have been small groups of itinerant singers, dancers and story-tellers. And we know that on important ecclesiastical holidays, or Holy Days—Christmas, Easter, or the feast of Corpus Christi—miracle or mystery plays were presented wherein religious stories like the Birth of Christ, Noah's Flood, the Fall of Adam and Eve, were dramatized and presented by craftsmen's guilds and other groups of the community.

The development of a secular drama was coincident with the Renaissance. As the power of the church declined, theatrical groups sought the patronage of royalty and great noblemen. But before long the writers and players began to realize that the function of a patron was unnecessary, that if their offerings were widely accepted, they could finance their own productions and live profitably off the proceeds. Ironically, Shakespeare, and the friends and partners with whom he worked, were the originators in England of the commercial theatre. The principle began to be established that drama was just one more commodity to be offered for sale. The more "popular" a play was, the more profitable would its production be. The dangerous distinction began to be apparent between merit, which is purely subjective and of which there are no objective standards of measurement, and popularity, which can be objectively and accurately measured in terms of receipts at the box office. It must have been almost immediately apparent that the most popular and successful plays are rarely those which appeal to the more discriminating members of a community, or which are apt to survive the moment of their original success. But by now the theatre, at all events in England, was irretrievably committed to a commercial policy.

In Europe the distinction was always more clearly preserved between a commercial and an artistic theatre. In France the Comédie Française has always been a subsidised institution, never wholly dependent upon popular favor, but dependent for its revenue upon maintaining a standard of taste and competence which seemed to redound to the credit of the community. In Germany the theatre has always been regarded as a necessity in a civilized community. Every city with the least pretension to culture has been willing to spend public money handsomely to assist dramatic and operatic art.

The English-speaking communities, however, are only beginning to feel this way. Theatre to them has never been accepted as an Art; it is merely Entertainment. And the view has been consistently held that if an entertainment cannot pay its way it cannot be any good. This view is still general in the United States. Great Britain, officially at all events, now thinks otherwise. In 1940, under the threat of war and fearing for the survival of cultural institutions, the British government took its first step toward the public subvention of the theatre. In return for sending a classical production (*Macbeth* with

Sir Lewis Casson and Dame Sybil Thorndike) to mining villages in South Wales and Northumberland, a limited guarantee against loss was offered to the Old Vic Theatre.

In a short time this tentative beginning was followed by bolder and more generous subsidy. Now, almost a quarter of a century later, the Arts Council of Great Britain gets from the treasury an annual grant of £2,730,000 (over seven and one-half million dollars).* The lion's share goes to the Royal Opera and Ballet at Covent Garden, to Sadler's Wells, and to the National Theatre, which now incorporates the Old Vic. But enough is left over to assist a number of smaller theatrical enterprises all over the country. Compared to the public subsidies available for drama in France, Germany or Russia, the amount is beggarly and represents but a faint and timid enthusiasm. It is, however, a beginning.

In the United States, on the other hand, government has as yet played no part in the encouragement of a less commercial attitude towards the drama. The matter is bedeviled by the conflict between Federal and State authority. However, so long as some of the great foundations are willing to shoulder the responsibility for artistic subsidy, there is less urgent need for public authorities to do so. However, even fortunes so vast as those of the Ford or Rockefeller Foundations cannot adequately supply the needs of a whole continent. Meantime there is no sign whatever that taxpayers would feel it their duty, let alone their pleasure, to relieve the foundations of the burden.

I think that there are two main reasons why the English-speaking communities feel so much less responsibility toward the arts than the French or Russians, Germans or Scandinavians.

First, both British and American culture has been heavily

---

* These figures are quoted from the report of the Arts Council of Great Britain for 1963–64. It should be borne in mind that the tendency is for each year's estimates to rise; and the annual subsidies available for the arts in France, Germany, and Russia, and almost all other European countries, are proportionally much larger than in Great Britain.

influenced by Puritan ideas of virtue—and of vice. To Puritans the theatre was, and is, at best a place of frivolous and expensive amusement, but far more often a sty of carnality. Actors and actresses, creatures who paint their faces, jig and amble, lisp and nickname God's creatures, are empty-headed and frequently licentious show-offs, anxious only for applause, unscrupulously greedy, incapable of serious thought or noble aspiration. Since Puritans are seldom widely read or widely experienced—reading and experience are great breeders of a tolerance which Puritans regard as laxity—it does not occur to them that there is a distinction between show business and the sort of theatre which is represented by Aeschylus, Shakespeare, Goethe, Ibsen, or Shaw. The whole jing-bang is written off, with a heroic disregard of all evidence to the contrary, as decadent foolery.

The result of this widespread Puritan attitude has been the relegation of drama to the category of commercial entertainment. Public money has been generously available for hospitals, schools and universities, for the maintenance of law and order, for scientific research and, of course, for the armed forces. It is not questioned that all these make for the public protection and betterment. Public money, in far smaller but nonetheless considerable amounts, has been available for libraries, art museums, and symphony orchestras. It is appreciated that good books are apt to be less profitable than trash, but should nevertheless be made available to the minority who want to read them. The same is true of paintings and music. It has not been the same with drama. Drama is not regarded as uplifting or educative, as conducive to wisdom and strength. It is merely "entertainment," and, therefore, to the Puritan, unworthy of serious consideration.

The second reason why drama has never been taken seriously by the English-speaking communities is because they are, like the Romans and unlike the Greeks, fundamentally philistine. Art and culture are regarded, on the whole, as being of no serious importance, as being no more than the pastime of rich, elderly ladies. The result has been that art in most English-speaking communities has been, not exclusively, but much too much concerned with courting the favor and avoiding the displeasure of these rich, elderly ladies. This has been especially the case in parts of the United States where these same rich, elderly ladies wield enormous economic bludgeons. On the whole, they do so with a great deal more discrimination and public spirit than the community has any right to expect. But inevitably the sort of "culture" which they foster is an expression of themselves rather than of the community at large; and the community is often apt to write off culture as a huge and un-American bore.

If you seriously doubt this, examine the amount of space in any, even the best, of the newspapers published in the English-speaking world. Compare the space devoted to literature, music, painting or drama with the space devoted to what people regard as seriously interesting: business, politics, sports and, as a bad fourth, religion. And compare the space devoted to these to what few care to admit is a serious interest—sex, as exemplified in the columns of police-court news, scandal and gossip columns. Finally, compare even the space devoted to these with the space devoted to the advertisements of commodities. It may be argued that newspapers derive their revenue from these advertisements. But doesn't the revenue naturally derive from what the public is most anxious to read about? If the public were principally interested in politics, religion or art and only marginally in commodities, newspapers would very soon have to reorganize their financial arrangements and their lay-out.

The Greek theatre was great not because a lucky chance produced a quick succession of four great dramatists. It was no lucky chance. The dramatists were the product of their time and their environment. There was a public, compact, highly sophisticated and articulate, ready to evoke the sort of drama which it wanted and needed. This sort of drama was *Prometheus Bound, Oedipus, Medea,* and *The Frogs.*

We have no analogous public. The sort of drama which the American public at present seems to want is the sort which it gets—from breakfast to bedtime, from cradle to grave—on commercial TV, the sort of drama which anonymous creatures called Sponsors think will sell soup and watch straps and armpit deodorants: *Gunsmoke,* in fact, and *Dr. Kildare.* But does anyone passionately want, really need, this sort of drama? We all know perfectly well that it is way below the level of the taste or the intellect of anyone who would take it seriously. It is not, in fact, taken seriously. It is just a very, very easy pastime for tired or bored people who are only prepared to give to it a low degree of concentrated attention.

And what of our contemporary professional theatre? It is organized as a business. Plays are expected to make money, and successful plays do so. Indeed a highly successful play on Broadway can give its backers a return of a thousand per cent on their investment. Unfortunately, very few plays are so successful. The vast majority go down with all hands and the loss of an Emperor's ransom. To make the money necessary to recover the costs of its production, the appeal of a successful play must be very wide. This means that it cannot be very deep. Now and again a seriously interesting play will also be popular, but the overwhelming majority of successful theatrical entertainments are either musicals which make not the least pretension to being other than appetizing bon-bons, or small comedies designed to while away the tedium between a heavy dinner and a boozy supper.

This state of affairs will continue until the public demands a more serious and mature kind of theatre. Actors and authors cannot create this demand. They can supply a demand, but they cannot create it. In my opinion, it cannot be created in the theatrical conditions of any modern metropolis. The audience is too disparate, too cosmopolitan. It no longer consists of neighbors with a common taste founded on community of experience and feeling. This is what the Athenian audience was, and its common experience and feeling had been refined and sharpened into the instrument which created the finest system of democratic government which has yet been known, a system of philosophy in advance of any but the most acute thinkers of subsequent ages, immeasurably ahead of the popular thought and feeling of our own time, and, finally, the taste which evoked architecture, sculpture and drama which have never since been surpassed. Probably it evoked music and painting of the same quality; unfortunately, as civilization progressed onward and upward, these expressions have been destroyed.

Why, you may be thinking, if Greek drama is so great is it so seldom seen? The answer is two-fold. First, even if we could experience it in its full glory, it would almost certainly be way above the heads of audiences organized, as ours are, under a commercial system. What was good enough for the Athenian audience then would be far too good for us now. Second, we cannot experience the full glory; we have to make shift with texts which are, in many instances, corrupt and incomplete, and, in all instances, they reach us only in translation. Inevitably, in any translation, much of the quality of a great original is lost; and especially is this the case with the translation of verse intended to be spoken.

Here and there a translator of genius will appear. For instance, the great Irish poet W. B. Yeats has translated the choruses of *Oedipus* into poems of his own; terse, powerful, musical and entirely free from the sentimentality which besets many translators of Greek verse. But, in general, these masterpieces reach us in translations which, striving manfully to capture meaning, have lost all melody. They are intelligible, of great interest to a student, but in performance they cannot burst into flame. Even for Greeks the original texts are hard to understand today. To modern Greek the classical texts bear about the same relation as Chaucer or Langland do to modern English.

We can see at Epidaurus, and one or two other places, fairly well-preserved architectural remains of classical Greek theatres. From these, as well as from evidence in the texts themselves and in the writing of eyewitnesses, we can piece together some notions of what the performances were like. But the notions are scanty, and the gaps in our knowledge are very wide. We know that masks and buskins were worn; we know that the choruses were accompanied by music and dancing. But we have no precise knowledge about the music or about the dancing, whether the choruses were completely sung, whether there was a mixture of singing, half-chanting and speech, whether the dancing was continuous or intermittent. We do not know how the principal actors, whom the best evidence places high on a raised platform or "proskenion," related themselves to the chorus below in the circular, and surprisingly large, "orchestra." If it is correct that the usual number of people in a chorus was fifteen, then, to fill so large a space as the orchestra at Epidaurus, the dancing must have been extremely nimble; and how do we reconcile this with the fact that quite often the chorus represented old men or women? In fact, the gaps in our knowledge are so large that all we can do is to use the light of our imagination—a flickering and feeble and misleading light—to interpret the plays as best we can.

I have seen two important festival performances in the great theatre at Epidaurus. In each case the sense of occasion was superb. To be part of an audience of fifteen thousand is, in itself, exciting. To be so, in these ancient and awesome surroundings, in this wild and desolate, ghost-haunted countryside, turns excitement to awe. To be part of an audience, unmistakably "popular" in character, humanizes the occasion; it is legendary, but real. To be sure, there were hundreds of tourists with their cameras, their thermos bottles, with cushions and insecticides to insure against discomfort and mosquitoes. But these were outnumbered twenty to one by Greeks, and not just smart intellectuals from Athens; this was an audience of neighbors. In spite of the tourists, in spite of the inevitably antiquarian and cultural overtones, most people had come for a night out, an excursion; many had come in donkey carts.

Around the outskirts of the vast arena were picnic parties on the mountainside.

The performance is timed to start as the sun drops below the jagged mountains to the northwest. I shall never, as long as I live, forget that moment. The sun goes down fast there, in a glory of orange, vermilion and crimson. The noise was gigantic—fifteen thousand or more, excitedly chattering in this immensely reverberant bowl. As the sun finally sank, so the sound drained away. In the space of ten or fifteen seconds the enormous, crashing reverberation died to the silence of death. Then one heard the cry of a night bird and the chirp of crickets. A man sitting beside me, with two sleepy and excited little boys, gathered them close to him and pointed, silently directing their attention to the stage. Arc-lights have come on. For a moment, they sizzle. Then silence again. An actor—peanut-sized—walks onto the stage. He is far, too far off for us to see what he really looks like. But—there!—you can hear—oh easily—the intake of breath before he speaks.

The stage has been "restored." A German-trained architect has erected in cement what looks like a crematorium. It is "monumentalisch" and, to my taste, vulgarly obtrusive.

The first performance which we saw was *The Bacchae* of Euripides performed by the Greek National Theatre. The principal actors spoke out good and loud and made big gestures as if they were doing Wagner. The operatic effect was reinforced by a live orchestra fiddling away like mad things inside the crematorium. The score had been specially composed for the occasion but had, I thought, more than a hint of Richard Strauss. Katina Paxinou played Agave. It is not the leading part, but Paxinou invested it with all the authority and force of a great actress. It was as if the play had been pushed a little to one side. The chorus had been trained by a German operatic choreographer; they tripped about in Greek-type poses to extremely un-Greek music. There was no suggestion of primitive and violent frenzy, these were not maenads but flower-girls from *Parsifal,* plumply, pinkly, invincibly respectable.

A week or so later, we saw *Helena,* also by Euripides, given by a much less celebrated ensemble. The performance was simpler and, to my way of thinking, a great deal better. The chorus' movements were derived from Greek folk dances and the music was provided by a sort of pipe-and-tabor. The acting was sufficient rather than resplendent. Neither Helen nor Menelaus quite suggested their timeless, archetypal greatness. But the play "went" splendidly. Where one could sense that the audience at *The Bacchae* was a little disappointed, this second audience was enchanted. The dénouement was greeted with a satisfactory volley of applause. This was no hyper-aes-thetic, over-awed reaction to a cultural masterwork; it was the healthy pleasure of ordinary people when love—and in this case mature, married love—laughs at locksmiths. And yet it was clear that, though this was a much better shot at the target than *The Bacchae,* it was still nowhere near the bull's-eye.

The best performance at Athens that summer was of *The Birds.* I have no idea what a serious student of Aristophanes would have made of it. But I do not see how he could disapprove of its being genuinely and charmingly funny. The acting was broad and noisy and the director was not ashamed to make use of some of the oldest gags in the business. This was as it should be. Aristophanes is one of the oldest gag-writers in the business. The production "went" like nobody's business. But I suspect that in London or New York it would be considered rather amateurish, rather "community theatre." So much the worse for London and New York. It was exactly this which gave it charm. Everyone knew everyone else. The actors knew just how to amuse this particular audience, as Shakespeare's actors knew just how to amuse the audience in London, and Mo-lière's how to amuse the Parisians. That does not seem to me to be amateurish. It is professional but in a different and, I think, better way than the glossy, impersonal efficiency which is de-manded now by metropolitan audiences.

London, New York, and Paris are now centers not primarily of theatrical art but of an entertainment industry. Rents are phenomenal because, if theatres are to continue to occupy metropolitan sites, they must produce a revenue commensurate with what the same sites would produce as offices, hotels or shops. Services in so competitive and crowded a market command wildly inflated prices. If it is to operate profitably, management must pass on these prices to the theatre-goer. The theatre-goer is therefore no longer the patron of an art, but the customer in a highly competitive, speculative luxury-trade.

If a theatre is ever to capture the kind of audiences which make for great drama, it must seek conditions which the great metropolitan centers can, in my opinion, no longer supply. It must go where competition for money is not so fierce; where real estate and services are not so expensive; where contact with neighbors can be freely established, man to man, as opposed to contact with plastic strangers effected, at enormous cost, through something called Public Relations. Furthermore, the sort of audience which will create a great theatre will, like the audience of classical Athens, go to the theatre not just as an idle pastime, to hear pretty music, to see pretty young things in pretty frocks and to laugh at comedians cracking jokes. The theatre will be a place of worship.

Naturally this does not mean that it will be monotonously, frowningly serious all the time. Serious purpose is perfectly compatible with humor; serious topics can be treated with wit. Through its mixture of philistinism and Puritanism, the American public has become conditioned to thinking of the theatre simply as frivolity. This impression will not be erased, be it admitted, so long as Broadway conducts its affairs with the crashing vulgarity which is at present considered to be good business. *The Matchmaker*, for instance, which ran for a very successful year and a half some seasons ago, and which is a gentle and wise expression of one of the great writers of our time, was advertised by a drawing of a saucy, sexy, little doll who was luring a lot of males, presented as prancing roosters, into a bird cage. This had no connection whatever with either the material or the spirit of the play. It was simply to convey the notion of hot stuff, the notion that a sexy, randy evening awaited the buyer of a ticket.

Of course not all plays are so advertised. But very many, even most, are. It is one instance of the kind of degradation which is inevitable when commercial ideas are dominant; when the criterion of merit is how many tickets you can sell.

Commercial ideas are now completely dominant in the large metropolitan cities, and have created conditions, material and spiritual, which in my view cannot be battled from within. It may be that commercial ideas will dominate everywhere. I do not believe so. Metropolitan theatre has decayed into mere showbiz, partly because of the inflationary conditions created by over-crowding and over-competition, but perhaps more because of the non-cohesive, transient and frivolous nature of metropolitan audiences. The audiences are no longer friends and neighbors bound by community of thought and feeling. The metropolitan cities are too large and loud; the ants who scurry about their streets are bewildered, too distracted by sound and fury, signifying nothing.

In Athens it is still possible for a theatre to survive. It is small enough. So is Dublin. So are Copenhagen, Oslo and Helsingfors; and, oddly enough, in all these cities the drama is lively. The liveliest theatre in France is no longer in Paris but in a suburb of Lyons where a genius called Roger Planchon has set up shop.

I do not foresee that New York has much more to contribute to a lively theatre. Showbiz has taken over. The new American theatre will arise elsewhere, and not, in my opinion, in any of the larger centers.

4. SHAKESPEARE ON STAGE

THE STAGE HISTORY of Shakespeare's plays has been greatly affected by the fact that even in his lifetime there was already brewing the strong Puritan reaction to drama which was to result, in 1642, in the banning of public theatrical performance for nearly a decade. When, after the restoration of the monarchy in 1660, the theatre came back it was a very different institution from that of Shakespeare's day. It is hard to believe that such a drastic revolution in dramatic taste, technique and philosophy could have occurred in less than 50 years.

We are apt to think that in our own age changes occur more rapidly and with more far-reaching effect than in any other. But I think all ages have felt the same. In our day the development first of movies, then of radio and television have brought immense changes in methods of distribution of drama. But, in fact, the very changed nature of theatrical business has, in my opinion, had surprisingly little effect on theatrical art. The difference between drama in 1947 and drama now in 1965 is nothing like so striking as that beween drama in 1642 and 1660.

One of the problems of the eighteen-year break in theatrical continuity, and of the astonishing change in theatrical taste which occurred at the same time, is that there exists no continuity of theatrical tradition. We do not, in fact, have more than an incomplete knowledge of how Shakespeare's plays were produced in his own lifetime. And our knowledge of the architecture of the theatres is likewise incomplete. It depends partly upon references in the texts of the plays—the opening chorus of *Henry V*, for instance, with its mention of a cockpit, and a wooden "O"—and partly upon a few engravings, which were intended to give a general impression but are far from reliable as detailed evidence. Indeed, the leading experts differ from one another considerably in many matters of important detail. But, in general, we do know that the Elizabethan stage stuck out into the middle of the auditorium. The audience sat and stood *around,* rather than just *in front of,* a raised platform. But this was not what we now call theatre-in-the-round. At the back of the stage there was a permanent architectural background, undoubtedly incorporating an upper level which could be used as a balcony (*Romeo and Juliet*) or a battlement, or for any purpose for which a second, elevated level might be useful. It is in connection with the space under this balcony that controversy rages. But the controversy is not relevant. For our purpose the facts to stress are that the players were *in the midst* of their audience, and that there were no realistic scenic indications. The whereabouts of characters was deduced from the text—"this castle hath a pleasant seat"—and the costume and demeanor of the players.

Further, the Elizabethan audience was a very democratic one. The upper-class had the privilege of the best seats, for which they paid quite high prices of admission. But in the same house there were lower-priced seats occupied by a less exclusive clientele, and the pit, on ground level, immediately surrounding the raised stage, was crowded by standees with no claims whatever to social importance. The audience was a full cross-section of society.

By 1665 the kind of play, the kind of audience, the whole purpose of drama were all radically different from what had prevailed in the last years of Queen Elizabeth's reign. And the difference was most strikingly expressed in theatrical architecture. The Restoration theatres were all built under the influence of the Italian opera, or musical works, which in the early seventeenth century had taken Europe by storm, sweeping away Renaissance conventions and conceptions of drama and replacing them with something more artificial, far less popular and more exclusive—a conception of Drama essentially urban, sophisticated and upper-class.

The seventeenth-century Italian opera house was in essence very much the same as a modern opera house. And the conventional design of all theatres has been based ever since upon that of the opera house. The audience sits facing the stage, in American houses usually on two levels—orchestra and balcony. European houses usually have two or even three balconies, one above the other. The stage faces the audience, but between it and the audience a great gulf is fixed. Practically, this gulf contains the orchestra; symbolically, it separates an upper-class audience from the churls who are paid to entertain. In addition to this spatial barrier there is a further, and even more symbolic, one of light and fire—the footlights. The stage is architecturally enclosed by a proscenium frame, on which hangs the curtain, behind which the stage "pictures" are prepared, and which rises (or draws) to disclose the semi-magical world of dramatic or operatic illusion . . . lo and behold!

Now for the Italian opera this is a logical and sensible arrangement. Practically, it enables the conductor, in the orchestra pit, to dominate both the orchestra and the singers on stage. The singers, brilliantly lit, face the darkened auditorium, and can be heard and seen to advantage, and are also conveniently placed to "see the beat." Theoretically, it is sensible too. Seventeenth-century operas aimed to create a highly artificial, elegant, illusionary world. The themes were largely mythological or allegorical—Daphnis and Chloe, Orpheus and Eurydice, Rinaldo and Armida, that kind of thing—in which the humanity of the personages was subordinate to elegance, grandeur and, above all, musical virtuosity. But, paradoxically, the thing about the proscenium stage which began more and more to enchant the public was not its elegant artificiality, but its ability to create a limited, but amusing, kind of realism—landscapes which gave a clever "illusion" of space and distance;

rooms, like dollhouse rooms, which were just like real rooms
except that everyone knew perfectly well that they were not
real rooms. Gradually, because of public demand, plays came to
be written to exploit this kind of realism; acting was scaled
down to life size; more and more merit came to be associated
with words like "natural," "life-like," "true."

Paradoxically, opera, for which the proscenium theatre had
come into being, began to change its nature. The highly-stylized
works of the seventeenth and eighteenth centuries became old-
fashioned. The public demanded more passion, ever more
elaborate spectacle. The paradox reached its height, as the
nineteenth century turned into the twentieth, with the so-called
verismo of Puccini—an attempt to introduce theatrical naturalism into the highly-stylized medium of sung drama. Puccini was
a genius and could just manage to achieve this all-but-impos-
sible feat. For instance, by setting it to highly charged, immensely skillful, emotional music, he transforms a very ordinary,
vulgar, commercial melodrama, by a highly-commercial New
York impresario called David Belasco, into a much higher
category of dramatic experience. *Madam Butterfly* is not a
masterpiece, or even nearly so, but it has triumphantly held
the stage for sixty years and will continue to do so for many
more—probably, as time goes on, in spite of, rather than because of, its *verismo*. Already the more realistic stage business,
and such lines as "have another whiskey and soda" tossed off
by a burly baritone, begin to seem absurd. But the emotional
force of the music purges away the grossness of the melodrama,
leaving the bones of a timeless, eternally poignant, situation.

But to return to Shakespeare. At the time of the Restoration—both of monarchy and drama—his plays had struck that
patch which inevitably awaits all works of art about thirty to
fifty years after their first vogue. They seemed "dated." Samuel Pepys, the diarist, found them artless and old-fashioned.
The end of the seventeenth century and the beginning of the
eighteenth was a period when other authors, notably Dryden

and Colley Cibber, made attempts to improve Shakespeare, to tidy up his straggling plots, to prune his rambling genius, to sophisticate his woodnotes wild. Partly the plays seemed dated because they were written for one kind of theatre and found themselves crammed into quite another kind of architectural framework, and partly because they were written for a particular kind of audience. By 1660 the theatre was aiming at quite another sort of public, and its whole purpose and philosophy had changed.

David Garrick, the great actor, in the middle of the eighteenth century was responsible for the restoration of Shakespeare's reputation as a great dramatist and the restoration of his texts to a form nearer, though not fully, that of the author's intentions. After Garrick there followed important Shakespearean revivals by Edmund Kean, William Charles Macready and Junius Brutus Booth—all showing marked respect for the poet's meaning. Macready, trying to reconcile Shakespeare and a stage now committed to realistic illusion, staged the plays with a great deal of attention to archaeological detail. Artists were sent to Italy to study architecture, light and landscape for the Italian romances, to Scotland for *Macbeth,* and one may suppose that some handsome and impressive, but not necessarily very relevant, effects were achieved.

Samuel Phelps' long management (1844–1862) at Sadler's Wells (twenty years and 34 of Shakespeare's plays) attracted the devoted attention of what we should now call a fan. He was a young city clerk called Brodribb, who eventually took his courage in both hands, shocking his family nearly to death, and went on the stage under the name of Henry Irving. After years of struggle and poverty he gradually made a sufficient reputation for himself to be able to choose plays and produce them under his own management. The result was the twenty-one years (1878–1899) of Irving's management of the Lyceum Theatre in London, during which a splendid series of productions was presented, predominantly but not exclusively Shakespearean. This period, largely because of Irving's enormous personal gifts as an actor, and possibly even more as a director, and because of his great personal prestige, saw Shakespeare finally re-established in London not just as an admired, but difficult and unpopular great author, but as a great box-office attraction. Incidentally, Irving, the first actor or theatrical person to receive the public recognition of knighthood, established for the first time in British history the respectability of the professional stage. Partly this was due to Irving's professional integrity and gifts of leadership, and partly it was because public opinion was becoming more liberal, more ready to believe that other activities besides politics, religion, business and warfare were serious.

But we are straying again from Shakespeare. Irving's productions were based on a realistic formula. There would be three or four splendid, elaborate "stage-pictures," and into these would be crammed as much of the action as possible. The scenes which simply could not be expressed realistically in these three or four environments were either cut or played as "front scenes." That is to say, a drop curtain would fall about six feet from the footlights, painted realistically to represent the front of an inn, a sea-coast, a garden or whatever might be required. The actors in such scenes had to play on a narrow shelf which prevented them from doing much more than coming on and standing in a row, like minstrels. They also had to holler good and loud in order to drown the hammerings and rumbles and curses of the stagehands as the next great stage-picture was being prepared behind the drop-curtain.

This, as Bernard Shaw never tired of writing in his brilliant criticisms, was butchering Shakespeare to make a stage-carpenter's holiday. But the method had several things to commend it: the stage pictures undoubtedly were very splendid. Irving hired good designers and was a master of lighting. The lighting, incidentally, was by gas, not electricity—a far softer and more controllable method of illumination, though the fire risks were hair-raising. Also, the public of that day absolutely demanded realism, in an elaborate, opulent style. And if this was to be supplied, I simply can see no alternative to Irving's method of three or four big set-pieces, eked out by front scenes. Remember how often the environment changes in a Shakespeare play. *Twelfth Night,* for instance, opens with five different scenes in the first seven minutes.

But after Irving, and incidentally after the introduction of photography—the death-knell of theatrical realism as well as of realistic painting—ideas of Shakespearean production began to change. Bernard Shaw's influence here was important, both on informed public taste and, more practically, on his close friend and collaborator, Harley Granville Barker. Barker's career was short but extremely influential. He directed a number of Shaw's plays and was quickly appreciated as an outstandingly talented and original director. His active career in London covered little more than a decade and he only put on two Shakespearean productions, *A Midsummer Night's Dream* and *The Winter's Tale.* Naturally, neither was a great success at the box office; they were too far advanced and controversial, but they fired the imagination of an influential minority. Henceforth the course of Shakespearean productions in Britain began to flow in a different direction.

Early in the 1914 war, Barker went to the United States. He married a rich woman and worked thereafter only very intermittently. His contribution to Shakespearean production was the restoration of the text to its rightful importance. There were no cuts for the sake of scenic convenience, no scrunching of important material into front scenes, no pauses between scenes. An almost completely uncut text ran continuously, except for one or two intermissions. He did not, however, abandon the picture frame or the pictorial idea. Instead of attempting a series of realistic pictures, he arranged the stage with a permanent set which attempted to express in a generalized way the atmosphere of the play and which had the necessary facilities—entrances, exits, different levels and so on—to enable the performance to proceed without interruptions.

Meantime a slightly older man than Barker had been making more drastic experiments on what I believe to be a more fully considered principle. This was William Poel (1852–1934). The principle which underlay his productions was that to present Shakespeare's plays one must, as nearly as possible, reproduce the sort of stage for which they were written. Poel was not nearly so gifted a director as Barker, nor so brilliant and charming a man. He never made much of a mark in the professional theatre, and his extremely interesting productions were acted by amateur or semi-amateur casts in church halls, inexpensively and not very glamorously adapted for sporadic matinees or Sunday evenings, when no more important business was afoot. For this reason, Poel's influence was far less immediate than Barker's and has, even yet, not been fully recognized. But I believe that he, if anybody, ought to be regarded as the founder of modern Shakespearean production.

Meantime commercial productions of Shakespeare continued to be presented in Irving's style; and the apex of realism was reached at His Majesty's Theatre in 1911 where in a production of *Midsummer Night's Dream* real live rabbits frisked around the Beerbohm Trees.

But all over Europe the avant-garde theatre, following the lead of avant-garde painting, and reacting against the advent of photography, was in full flight in many directions, all headed away from opulent and elaborate realism. The most influential authors of this avant-garde theatre in the early years of this century were probably August Strindberg, Maurice Maeterlinck, and Gabriele D'Annunzio, and the most influential director was Jacques Copeau at his beautiful little theatre in Paris, Le Vieux Colombier. But we must not forget that the two theatres of this period which have exercised the greatest influence on our own epoch were not especially avant-garde, and were pledged in both cases to ideas which, to the avant-garde in 1905, seemed out of date. I refer to the ideas of creating a specifically national drama in an even more realistic if less opulent style than that of the commercial and fashionable stage. And the two

theatres were the Moscow Art Theatre under Konstantin Stanislavsky and the Abbey Theatre in Dublin under Lady Gregory
and W. B. Yeats.

Again we are straying away from Shakespeare, but Shakespearean production does not operate in a vacuum. All the
time it is being influenced by the general prevailing cultural
climate and by the particular trends and fashions of theatrical
productions.

I can dwell here only upon Shakespearean production in
Britain. It would take too long to cover the whole international
field. In Germany there have always been far more Shakespearean productions, but they have tended to remain far longer in a
nineteenth-century romantic style—often very splendid and
excellent—but surprisingly remote from the rest of contemporary expression. Partly this is because Shakespeare is still
almost entirely played in the Schlegel-Tisch translations made
in the romantic early days of the nineteenth century. Many
Germans maintain that these translations are better than
Shakespeare. No one maintains that they are very like Shakespeare. They are as though Shakespeare had been rewritten
by Shelley or Keats. Partly, German productions have remained
longer in the romantic style of the early twentieth century because of the overwhelming directorial influence of Max Reinhardt, which still dominates the classical theatre of central
Europe, but which was essentially an opulent, early twentieth-
century, naturalistic approach to Shakespeare.

In the United States no recognizably American style of
classical productions has yet emerged. Classical revivals on any
scale rely heavily upon European actors in the leading parts.
The American theatre has to its credit many true achievements
in the field of modern bourgeois and proletarian drama; it
excels in the production of light sentimental song-and-dance
shows. It will not, in my opinion, make much of a showing in
classical drama until American education is less obsessed with
training people to be economically successful and until more
attention is paid to language, literature and philosophy.

In 1919, after the war, the director of the Old Vic in London was a young Welshman named Robert Atkins. He was a disciple of William Poel and he collected around him a group of interesting, lively young veterans of the First World War. There resulted a splendid series of productions in which vigor and intelligence more than compensated for the extreme simplicity forced upon them by the theatre's penury. They attracted a great deal of favorable attention and, as a result, the Old Vic emerged from being a well-intentioned charitable enterprise into being one of the liveliest theatres in the world —a position maintained until 1963, when its identity was merged in that of the British National Theatre. Atkins adapted the principle of William Poel as well as he could to the existing plant of the Old Vic—a biggish, well-designed early nineteenth-century opera house. A great deal of compromise and make-do was necessary, as I discovered when, some fifteen years after Atkins' regime, I came to work at the Old Vic. Production after production seemed bedevilled by the shifts and compromises necessary to squeeze a play written for one kind of stage onto another, and, I felt, far more cramping kind of stage. Gradually, I became convinced that no radical advance in the production of Shakespeare would be possible until we could create a stage which resembled, far more nearly than the Old Vic or any other proscenium theatre, the sort of stage for which the plays were written. This conviction was strengthened by two experiments.

In 1936 the Old Vic was invited to take a production of *Hamlet* to Elsinore, in Denmark, where the action of the story is supposed to have really taken place. The whole thing was no more, in fact, than a stunt arranged by the Danish Tourist Board. But with Laurence Olivier as Hamlet and Vivien Leigh as Ophelia it was attracting a good deal of attention, and the opening was being attended by royalty, the *corps diplomatique* and representatives of the international press.

On the opening night it rained as it can have seldom rained since Noah's flood. The courtyard of the castle, where the performance was to take place, was exposed to the elements. Cancellation was impossible. The special train conveying the royal and distinguished guests had already left Copenhagen, so we decided to give the performance in the ballroom of a hotel. While Laurence Olivier and the company hastily re-arranged the choreography, I and the dramatic critics of *Paris-Soir* and the London *Daily Telegraph* re-arranged the ballroom with a clear space in the center of a thousand basket chairs.

The performance was inevitably something of a shambles, but I felt that it confirmed my belief about staging Shakespeare. With more time, *Hamlet* would have worked better in the freer surroundings of the ballroom than it ever could on a proscenium stage. Since at that time there was not the faintest possibility of reconstructing the Old Vic, these ideas had to remain unrealized. But about ten years later I was asked to direct, for the Edinburgh Festival, a sixteenth-century Scottish play called *The Three Estates*. It is in very broad, archaic Scottish dialect and is a highly allegorical morality-piece about God and man. It seemed to me utterly unfeasible to put it onto a proscenium stage, but I thought it might work with the far freer, broader, less realistic treatment which an open stage permits. We staged it in the middle of a large, square, galleried hall, and thanks to the splendidly vigorous performance of the Scottish actors it was a resounding success. I now felt convinced that for plays written before about 1640, the open stage was the answer.

Opportunity to put this belief to yet another test came when, in 1951, I was asked to be the artistic director of the Shakespeare Festival at Stratford, Ontario, in Canada. I accepted on condition that the plays could be produced on an open stage. The committee agreed and hired my old friend and collaborator Tanya Moiseiwitsch to design a stage which would implement the theories which she and I had for years been discussing and which we had both been longing to try. I think the success of the Festival vindicated our belief. And, while I would not know how successfully my own productions realized our theories I do know that on this Canadian stage my successor as Artistic Director, Michael Langham, has done a series of Shakespearean productions which are, in my opinion, the most consistently interesting and exciting of our time.

What are the particular advantages of this open stage? First, a theatre built on this plan with the stage sticking out into the midst of the house and the audience sitting around, though not behind it—such a theatre makes more economic use of cubic space than a theatre built on the operatic or proscenium plan. The theatre at Stratford holds something over 2,000 people; but if the seats were arranged to face a proscenium, it would barely hold 1,200. The new theatre at Minneapolis, where I am currently engaged, holds 1,450 people and looks and feels as intimate as a proscenium house of about 800 capacity.

This means that the contact between actors and spectators is more intimate. More than that, the more densely the cubic space of an auditorium is filled with people, the higher is the voltage such an audience generates. This is an all-important feature of theatrical design of which all performers are acutely aware, but which modern architects are apt to overlook. There is evidence that the Globe Theatre, built by the company of which Shakespeare was one of the directors and principal stockholders, held 3,000 people. For its size this was a phenomenal capacity, only achievable because in the pit, the area on ground level nearest to the stage, the spectators stood and were not provided with seats. Of course, no modern audience would tolerate this; any more than we would tolerate exposure to the weather, even showery London weather. But we carry the pursuit of comfort too far. It is possible to be too comfortable. Ultimately physical comfort leads to somnolence, not alertness. Also it is a fact that we value something more if we pay dear for it whether in money or physical comfort.

The next advantage of the open stage for Shakespeare is that it suits the text. It was the way the author imagined his plays. When it is necessary that the audience should know the whereabouts of characters or the setting of events, this information is invariably given in the text, usually in a passage of memorably vivid description. Take Lorenzo's speech to Jessica about the night sky, in the *Merchant of Venice*. The environment—a moonlit garden—is all evoked by the words. If they are musically spoken it is not only superfluous but boring and vulgar to attempt visual illusion with black velvet and sequins. In *Macbeth* it is desirable to know that Macbeth's castle "hath a pleasant seat," that here the temple-haunting martlets, or swallows, build their nests. It is described at some length in the text to make the ironic point that this pleasant and peaceful environment is about to be the scene of a ghastly regicide. Shakespeare's verbal description is designed with masterly economy to evoke the scene musically by verbal association. What is gained by an elaborate structure in 3-ply and chicken wire, covered with artificial foliage? It merely mocks the poet's intention and flaunts its own ineptitude.

Absence of scenery enables the plays to proceed, as their author intended, from scene to scene without the slightest break in continuity. Breaks—while an orchestra tries ineffectually to drown the noise and bustle of a scene change, while the audience sits in an uneasy darkness and while any tension generated by the preceding scene evaporates before the next one has begun—such breaks undermine some of Shakespeare's most thrilling and best calculated effects, which depend upon the immediate juxtaposition of scenes, fast with slow, loud with soft, grave with gay, grand with squalid.

Finally, the fact that an audience sits *around* the stage makes it easier to apprehend what is, in fact, the purpose of theatrical performance. The proscenium stage encourages us all to believe that this purpose is to create illusion. I do not believe that audiences above the age of eight years old are illusionized. They do not mistake a palpable fiction for fact. They do not believe that the good-humored little lady suspended, in acute discomfort, on an easily visible wire is Peter Pan. They know perfectly well that she is Mary Martin.

The open stage, on the other hand, positively discourages illusion. You can hardly suppose you are in the Bower of the Fairy Queen or on a blasted heath in the highlands of Scotland when across the stage you can descry—in a dim light, to be sure, far dimmer than that which illuminates the actors—the McKinstrys, who live on the next block, and, a little to the right, dear old Miss Halverson, who keeps the corner store. Some people may find this disturbing. I think it is just right. It reminds us of two important facts about theatrical performance. First, its object is not to create the illusion that a palpable fiction is a fact, but rather to recreate in ritual terms an ordered and significant series of ideas. Secondly, it is essentially a sociable, communal affair. This is important. By being a member of an audience one surrenders some of one's own individuality. One's own personality becomes fused in the mass-personality. To resist this is, I think, to ruin one of the very important parts of the theatrical experience. Let the play and let the fact that temporarily you are not your private self, but a member of a closely-fused group, make it easy for the performance to "take you out of yourself." This, I suggest, is the object of going to a play . . . to be taken out of yourself, out of your ordinary life, away from the ordinary, and frequently rather drab and dismal world of everyday.

But being taken "out of yourself," or "rapt," or "transported" is not to be confused with being "taken-in" by an illusion. You can be transported and still know perfectly well that the play is not really happening, still preserve a perfectly clear distinction between fact and fiction, illusion and reality. Take the analogy of other arts. Does anybody expect that a performance of a symphony will create illusion? Of course not. But a musical person is, none the less, easily transported by good performance of good music. When you read a good novel do you believe that you are right there on the desert island with Robinson Crusoe? Or on Main Street with Babbitt and the Rotarians? Of course not. You know perfectly well that you are in your chair in the living room. The fact that your imagination has been temporarily, and totally, engaged in the fiction does not imply that you have not been aware of it as fiction, that you have assumed it to be fact.

So with the theatre.

The quality of the theatre's fictions varies widely. Shakespeare's are generally acknowledged to be of high quality. His characters express with matchless vividness and often with blinding accuracy and simplicity an extraordinarily wide range of ideas and emotions. The characters themselves cover a wide range—from tiny, touching vignettes of unimportant sillies to great towering symbolic embodiments of the human predicament, such as Hamlet, Lear or Macbeth. I feel strongly that we must present them in such a way that they are not reduced to naturalistic portraits of real people. They are not real or natural or ordinary. They are the prodigious creations of genius —larger, louder, brighter-colored than the people we meet in the post-office or on the bus. They are, in my opinion and for the reasons I have stated, better presented on an open stage, right out among the audience, than within a proscenium, cut off by curtain, footlights and orchestra-pit, from the spectators.

This is not to say that splendid performances of Shakespeare have not been given, and will not in future be given, on proscenium stages. Nor is it to say that the open stage is the right kind of stage for every kind of play. I say no more than that, in my opinion, the open stage makes the presentation of Shakespeare easier for the actors and a more vivid experience for the audience, and that, again in my opinion, the return to the sort of stage which Shakespeare had in mind when he wrote his plays is a most important advance in Shakespearean interpretation.

5. HIDDEN MOTIVES IN FIVE SHAKESPEAREAN PLAYS

Hamlet

Hamlet is always going on somewhere.

Hardly a week passes but I get a letter from some well-meaning person who has seen a school performance in Wichita, Brisbane, Middlesborough, Aughnacloy or Medicine Hat, and the fourteen-year-old Hamlet has been so marvelous, so truly extraordinary, that the writer is absolutely certain that if I would just take the trouble to make the few practical arrangements necessary to present young Smith, or Brown, in a professional production. . . .

The fascinating thing is that young Smith, or Brown, probably *was* marvelous. The play is so spellbinding, the part is so grateful and so dominates the evening, that it is quite hard not to seem marvelous if you play it. I have seen about a hundred productions of *Hamlet,* ranging from very high, metropolitan and professional standards down to efforts in church basements by Women's Rural Institutes; not even the feeblest of them failed to throw fresh illumination upon some points, none were so raw and crude as totally to obscure the greatness of the play. An official of a large public library in England once told me that books about the lives of three men were statistically in a class by themselves. Where other lives were borrowed by tens, these three were borrowed by hundreds. The three in statistical order of importance were the lives of Jesus Christ, Hamlet, and Napoleon Bonaparte.

This evidence suggests that the character of Hamlet has an extraordinary validity and vitality. Not only is his biography of interest to an enormous number of readers, but it has lured into print an enormous number of authors. Their views about his character and the meaning of the play which bears his name are, considering the fact that all are arguing from the same evidence, quite astonishingly various.

The same divergence of interpretation is apparent in the theatre. John Gielgud's Hamlet is an entirely different sort of man from the Hamlet of Maurice Evans, with the result that the play has one kind of meaning when Gielgud plays and an entirely different meaning, even a different kind of meaning, when Evans plays. I suppose the possibility of great divergence of meaning is one of the distinguishing features of a masterpiece: it denotes a certain richness. One performance of *Oklahoma!* cannot differ very much from another. One may be better mounted, acted and sung, and may thus increase the enjoyment of the audience, but it will not offer a very different *kind* of experience. It cannot greatly alter the meaning of a work, which, for all its charm and freshness and verve, does not even pretend to have a great deal of meaning. Also, in the theatre, the meaning of a work will be more changed by the personality of the leading performer, if, as is notably the case in *Hamlet,* there is a single overwhelmingly important central character. But the matter of an actor's personality does not arise in the study. Even in seclusion, undistracted by the glamor and force of an actor's interpretation, readers of *Hamlet* arrive at startlingly divergent opinions about the meaning of the play and the significance, or relative importance, of all its characters and scenes.

But, it may be argued, *Hamlet* must have had one particular and precise meaning for the author. Therefore the reader in the study, or actors in the theatre, who most nearly approximate to that meaning are most nearly right. According to this argument it should theoretically be possible to achieve a right interpretation.

Superficially this seems reasonable; but, in fact, I think it implies a misunderstanding of the processes of artistic creation and interpretation. It is highly improbable that Shakespeare had a precise intention, and impossible, in the regrettable absence of the only witness in possession of the evidence, to determine what it was. If Shakespeare had a precise intention, then it must have been related to a particular context. He must have had in mind a particular actor at least for Hamlet, if not others for the King, Queen, Polonius and so on down to the officers who finally bear Hamlet off the stage. He must have had in mind a precise *mise en scène* for every moment of every scene, a precise rhythm, inflection, emphasis and color for every syllable of every speech, and a particular audience with whose tastes he was so familiar that its every reaction could be predicted.

No dramatic author can possibly think in these precise terms. He knows perfectly well that he is one of quite a large group of collaborators. His is certainly, and by far, the most important contribution to the collaboration, but allowance has to be made for the comment which will be made by director, designer, each actor and, not least, each member of each audience. No dramatic author, least of all if, like Shakespeare, he is an experienced and keen theatrical business man, will write with just one performance, one actor, one audience, one set of circumstances in mind. He will know that precision of intention, precision of meaning, can hardly be achieved in a single word, let alone a single sentence. It is totally impossible in a great complex of thought and feeling, action and reaction like *Hamlet,* which has to be interpreted by a whole group of collaborators to any Tom, Dick or Harry who happens to have paid for a seat.

Therefore, while it is obvious that Shakespeare must have had some meaning in mind when he wrote *Hamlet,* I think it is no less obvious that this meaning was not precise, and probably not even fully communicable. It is less obvious but still true that what Shakespeare consciously intended to write was far less important than what crept in between the lines of the text without his meaning it to be there—the "over and above," which differentiates art from craftsmanship.

In my view the conscious intention was no more than to dish up a version of a very unsophisticated but popular old play about murder and revenge in such a manner as to make it acceptable to his much more sophisticated but still popular audience. The plot was made more complicated, the motivation more subtle, the setting, the manners and the idiom were brought up to date. I cannot for one instance credit that Shakespeare was consciously writing for all eternity. Had he been doing so, it is inconceivable that he would not have taken the trouble to see that his work was carefully preserved in print. In fact so little was he interested in his plays as literature that when, some years after his death, his friends Heminge and Condell tried to get together a collection of his works for publication, they had the utmost difficulty in finding texts; and much of what they printed had obvious omissions and mistakes.

Is it not more reasonable to suppose that on the conscious level, Shakespeare, the keen business man, as we know him to have been, wrote an effective melodrama, set in the glamorous surroundings of a Royal Court, heavily laced with sex, with a spook and plenty of exciting action to grip and hold the attention of the customers? He cannot have supposed that the central figure in this farrago would be a topic of dispute for centuries, not only in England or even in English, but in all languages and every part of the civilized world.

Surely there is only one reason for this: any author must put into the creation of a very long, complex fictional character, like Hamlet, a great deal of himself—not merely the astute observations of a good journalist, not merely the conscious views of an experienced man of the world, nor the reflections of a wise philosopher, but his deepest feelings and intuitions (rather than rational reflections) about man's predicament in this mysterious and often apparently hostile universe. Shakespeare was not only an experienced man of the world, a brilliant journalist and a wise philosopher, he not only had a range of feeling and sympathy far, far beyond the ordinary—he was a poet. This means that instinctively his thoughts and feelings were not only expressed with clarity and simplicity but also in a memorable and musical form.

This is not to say that there are no poetic techniques. Poetry is not solely instinctive. No one who is not a poet can, by taking pains, even infinite pains, become one, any more than a non-musical person can become a musician. Infinite pains will enable him to master the technique of the violin or the piano or of theory of composition. Hitting, scraping or writing the correct notes does not produce music. Equally, there are multitudes of potential artists who, through lack of technique, because their gifts have never been educated, are doomed to be mute inglorious Miltons, Beethovens, Titians who never made a mark more interesting than the cross laboriously scrawled on their last will and testament. Shakespeare, fortunately for himself and more fortunately for us, had both the gift and the technique. The one would have availed little without the other. With both he was able to create *Hamlet,* but—and this is my contention—he no more consciously planned this great piece of poetic, psychological, theatrical and philosophic design than a nightingale plans the melody, rhythm and color of those notes which ravish the summer darkness.

Now, although there can never be a completely right way of interpreting *Hamlet,* there are many partly wrong ones, and the wrongest, I would say, are those which are demonstrably at odds with the text. Among these are the views of three of the most eminent literary critics of the early nineteenth century—Goethe, Schlegel and Coleridge—whose great reputations persuaded many people for a long time to agree with their views.

I think that almost everybody who studies *Hamlet* must agree that one thing about the play is especially puzzling:

Prince Hamlet, overwhelmingly conscious of the wrongs done to him by his uncle—the usurpation of the kingdom, the incestuous marriage with Gertrude, the murder of his father—overwhelmingly urged to revenge by his father's ghost, is still unable, though apparently not unwilling, to obey the ghost. Early nineteenth-century writers and critics were much concerned with morality. Characters were classified as Good and Bad; there was a tendency to oppose Heroes and Villains. The heroes were thought of as pure; the villains were compounded of almost unmixed evil. The great critics of the early nineteenth century were greatly concerned to show that Hamlet was "good." It was necessary to show that the play represented a conflict of good and evil, with good as nearly as possible victorious. Hamlet's indecision was, fairly enough on the evidence, attributed to qualms of conscience at avenging one murder by another. But it was clearly felt that there was something a little unheroic, a little effeminate even, in such niceties. One of Sir Walter Scott's heroes would not thus have quailed, nor would the heroes of medieval or classical legend. An explanation was sought and found, again in the verbal evidence of the play, but unfortunately not congruent to its events, in terms of action being "sicklied o'er by the pale cast of thought."

Goethe writes that "a lovely, pure and most moral nature, without the strength of nerve which forms a hero, sinks beneath a burden which it cannot bear and must not cast away." Schlegel describes Hamlet as "thought-sick" and considers that the whole play "is intended to show how a calculating consideration which aims at exhausting, so far as human foresight can, all the relations and possible consequences of a deed, cripples the power of action." Coleridge, traveling along the same lines, finds in Hamlet "an almost enormous intellectual activity and a proportionate aversion to real action consequent upon it."

When these three great dogs barked in unison, smaller dogs felt some reluctance to yap their disagreement. It was not until much later in the century that dissent was really expressed, based on the repeated evidence of the text itself. So strong, however, was the credit attached to the Goethe-Schlegel-Coleridge axis that, as late as the mid-nineteen forties, a film version of *Hamlet* made by Laurence Olivier was based on the premise that "This Is the Story of a Young Man Who Could Not Make Up His Mind." Unfortunately for itself, though maybe fortunately for the truth, the film made absolute nonsense of its premise, for it showed a person of formidably, if irrelevantly, Aryan blondness, who shouldered aside all opposition with splendid vigor, but paused now and again to say a few reflective words which were completely at odds with the appearance and behavior of their speaker. Without meaning to do so, the film refuted finally the Goethe-Schlegel-Coleridge view on which it was based. How could Hamlet be irresolute or incapable of action in view of the determined and efficient way in which he was seen to carry through the intrigue with the Players, the ruthless break with Ophelia, the forcible interview with his mother, the stabbing (albeit mistaken as to the victim's identity) of Polonius, the hoisting of Rosencrantz and Guildenstern with their own petard, the grapple with the pirates, the struggle with Laertes in Ophelia's grave?

Surely all these episodes are designed by Shakespeare to show that Hamlet is not only highly intelligent, but also a resolute and capable man, rendered irresolute and incapable by self-conflict, by qualms of conscience, only in the single matter of avenging his father's death by the murder of his uncle. This self-conflict is fascinatingly explained by Dr. Ernest Jones, the British psychoanalyst and biographer of Freud. His *Hamlet and Oedipus* brings psychoanalysis to bear upon both these masterpieces, and offers what is to me, by far, the most interesting and convincing explanation of the crucial puzzle of the play, Hamlet's procrastination in the matter of vengeance. Since Ernest Jones is concerned to show that Hamlet was inhibited by a conflict within himself of which he was not aware, his interpretation offers little which can be expressed in the theatre.

An intelligent actor does not require a professional analyst to tell him that his mother's over-hasty marriage with Uncle Claudius is a major emotional problem for Hamlet, nor that the great scene of recrimination with his mother is violently ambivalent (love and hate mixed), nor that Hamlet's explanation of the reason why he failed to destroy Claudius at his prayers is almost certainly a rationalization of more profound, but unconscious, motives.

It has been argued that Jones' interpretation cannot be right since Shakespeare, not having been privileged to live, like ourselves, in the age of Freud, knew nothing of the Oedipus complex. This argument is analogous to saying that a citizen of Athens in the age of Pericles would have thought it safe to jump off a high tower because the law of gravity had not yet been propounded. The phenomena of the Oedipus complex were observable, and Shakespeare observed and recorded them, three centuries before Freud isolated, analyzed and explained them. It is only natural that *Hamlet* should be interpreted by all sorts of people according to their various kinks and bends. There have, of course, been Marxian interpretations and I do not doubt that many people see in it little but a confirmation of their own views about Christian Science, bimetallism, the Monroe Doctrine, monogamy, vegetarian diet or spelling reform.

For my own part, I am particularly interested by a scene which, in the theatre, comes too late in the evening to get from a tired audience the attention which it might otherwise command. In the interim after Osric's departure, before Claudius and the court assemble for the sword-play between Hamlet and Laertes, there is a little scene between Hamlet and Horatio. Hamlet confesses to a strange feeling of misgiving: "Thou would'st not think how ill all's here about my heart." Then again a moment later, "But it is such a kind of gaingiving as would perhaps trouble a woman." Horatio begs him to excuse himself from the sword-play: "If your mind dislike anything, obey it. I will forestall their repair hither and say you are not fit." "Not a whit," replies Hamlet, "we defy augury; there is special providence in the fall of a sparrow." In other words, what must happen will happen, because it has been providentially foreordained.

Then follows a most enigmatic passage which has provoked a wide variety of interpretation: "If it be now, 'tis not to come; if it be not to come, it will be now; if it be not now, yet it will come: the readiness is all. Since no man has aught of what he leaves, what is't to leave betimes?"

"It" in this passage refers, I take it, to the fall of a sparrow, by which Hamlet refers to his own impending fall. The whole passage implies that he is aware that his own death is very near and is predestined, and that he accepts this situation: the readiness is all. The "gaingiving," the strange feeling about the heart, are the physical and emotional reactions to this certainty of presentiment. I think that I have experienced a similar feeling when an idea, or group of ideas, suddenly comes to my consciousness after no apparent process of reasoning or search. It is thus, in my experience, that all the really important decisions of a life are made. It may be the sudden blinding certainty which swept over Paul on the road to Damascus; it may be the quiet catch at the heart, the gaingiving of Hamlet. Decision may seem to be a rational process, but only a fool will make an important decision without being impelled by the revelation of new and determinant nonrational factors in the conglomeration of rational pros and cons.

Consideration of this passage makes me wonder whether this aspect of determinism may not be an important key to the mystery of Hamlet's procrastination. Shakespeare must have realized that great steps are seldom, if ever, taken by a conscious effort of will, but only when (usually through a conjunction of outward circumstances, as is the case in *Hamlet*) a decision simply cannot any longer be postponed. Even if Shakespeare had not perceived this phenomenon in his own experience, or that of his immediate circle, he can hardly have failed to notice it in the life of the most conspicuous figure of his day—Queen Elizabeth.

Elizabeth, like Hamlet, was brilliantly gifted, highly educated and highly strung; but, again like Hamlet, she was a resolute and capable person. Yet in two issues of dominant importance, both to herself privately and to the safety and health of the whole realm—her marriage and her foreign policy— she procrastinated, rationalized her indecisions and changes of mind, heard attentively and fearfully, but disregarded, the promptings of her father's ghost, whether it spoke through the mouth of her real father, Henry VIII, or through Lord Burleigh, the father-figure. Eventually decisions were taken out of her hands; she was forced, like Hamlet, by circumstance, or providence, into courses of action which turned out well for England, ill for Spain. In this connection let us note a point which Salvador de Madariaga makes: Hamlet did not so much fail to act as postpone action. He waited, like Elizabeth, until the moment for action had been clearly revealed.

I am not for a moment suggesting that in *Hamlet* Shakespeare was composing an analogue of the Virgin Queen, but merely that there was a conspicuous, literally unmissable, instance before Shakespeare's eyes of the paradox which is so striking in *Hamlet:* the capable and decisive person who is unwilling, perhaps even unable, to take decisive action in matters of the very highest private and public importance.

The little scene with Horatio marks the precise moment when, not suddenly or violently, but with a feeling of unmistakeable foreboding, Hamlet realizes that the decision has already been reached. He does not know how events will turn out, but the crisis is *now,* and it is inevitable. Further, and this is what seems to me so interesting, he realizes that providence, and not himself, is in charge. There is a providence in the fall of a sparrow; there's a divinity that shapes our ends, rough-hew them how we will. It is not a new idea in the play. He has implied it before. After the unintended murder of

Polonius, he looks at the body and says to his mother: "For this same lord, I do repent; but Heaven hath pleas'd it so, To punish me with this, and this with me, That I must be their scourge and minister."

He regards himself as a passive instrument in the hands of divinity and refuses, despite agonies of self-reproach and self-conflict, to allow the vindictive Ghost to hustle him into a conscious decision.

One small point, which I have never encountered in any of the commentaries. It concerns the name Polonius. It may not be of the highest significance, but it offers a clue to the way in which the part should be played. Polonius, I assume, is not so much a surname as a title, bestowed by Hamlet's father upon his chief counselor in recompense for his share in the victory over the Polack. Polonius is thus analogous to the title Coriolanus bestowed by the Roman Senate upon Caius Marcius to commemorate his victory over the Volscians and capture of their city, Corioli; analogous, in more recent time to the title Lord Kitchener of Khartoum bestowed after the Mahdi rebellion in the Sudan, Lord French of Ypres after World War I or Viscount Montgomery of Alamein. If this be accepted, then Polonius must be played as a very shrewd personage indeed, beginning possibly to show his age by being a little garrulous and tactless, but absolutely not a foolish or incompetent old man.

Coriolanus

Coriolanus is not often produced.

Why is this?

It has a splendid leading part, in which the extrovert brilliance of an important actor can be brilliantly deployed. It has a magnificent part for a senior lady, quite as good as Juliet's Nurse, better than Paulina in *Winter's Tale,* Katherine of Aragon, or The Countess Roussillon in *All's Well That Ends Well*. It is one of Shakespeare's least untidily constructed plays (though this author can never expect high marks for neatness) as well as one of his most vigorously theatrical. What is the deterrent?

I personally am always a little put off by Roman dress. It may be becoming—I guess it is—to those of perfect physique, but the ordinary mortal does not look well with skinny arms and legs thrusting out of a metal corselet. Greaves and armlets do not conceal but accentuate muscular shortcomings, and if, instead of armor, togas are worn, everyone seems to be scurrying about on Ladies' Night at the Turkish Bath. Yet Roman dress seems no deterrent to the production of *Julius Caesar,* one of the most frequently performed of Shakespeare's plays; and anyway, it is not necessary to play *Coriolanus* in Roman dress. It could, in my opinion, perfectly well be given in Elizabethan or in modern dress, or, even better, as in a spendid production by Michael Langham at Stratford, Ontario, in the period of Napoleon Bonaparte.

I think a likelier reason for the play's neglect is the fact that none of its chief characters are very "sympathetic." There is a theory in the modern theatre, and particularly in New York, that an audience expects to "identify with"—a barbarous phrase—certain aspects of the characters in a play or a novel. In *Coriolanus* there is no one with whom right-minded members of either sex would normally wish to identify. Coriolanus is far too big for his breeches, and eventually turns out to be a bad egg. Aufidius is a bad egg too. Menenius is a fuddy-duddy, a nice enough old person but there is nothing in him with which anyone under a hundred and eleven years old could identify. The Tribunes? Well, after all the scandal about the Teamsters Union, let's face it! no one much wants to identify with a Tribune. Of the ladies, Volumnia is a battle-axe, Virgilia the most colorless of namby-pambies, and Valeria so small a part as not to appear in the identification parade.

For my part I do not subscribe to the notion that audiences

want to identify. I do not believe that to enjoy *Hamlet* you have to undergo the absurd delusion that *you,* a necktie salesman, just wild about your stamp collection and a brunette named Shirley with cute hips, or *you,* a Presbyterian minister's widow in a small apartment in Flatbush . . . that either of you is under the absurd delusion that *you* are Hamlet. I do not believe that, to succeed, a play or story must be peopled with sympathetic characters. Becky Sharp is not sympathetic, but she is interesting, and that makes her better company than that goody-goody bore Amelia Sedley, with whom Thackeray intended his female readers to identify. Macbeth and Lady Macbeth are not sympathetic, nor is Peer Gynt, nor Harpagon in *The Miser.* Regina, in *The Little Foxes,* is not sympathetic. Yet the lack of sympathetic central characters has not come between any of these plays and their audience.

Can the difficulty be that the play's politics are unacceptable? Shakespeare, as always, takes no side in the controversy which he presents. The better educated upper-classes put their case more eloquently, and in the case of Menenius with humor; but the Tribunes speak up clearly and well and are allowed dignity in their final scenes of defeat, when, with Coriolanus at the gates, their enmity to him seems to have brought disaster upon Rome.

I suspect that since the re-emergence of Shakespeare as an important and successful dramatist—namely since about the 1700's—the excessive arrogance of Coriolanus may have seemed less credible and more unsympathetic than it did to Shakespeare's contemporaries a hundred years before. Audiences have become more and more politically inclined towards the tribunes' views, more and more unsympathetic toward the patricians. With the passing of more years this will become even more the case. Audiences are better at feeling than thinking. They are also creatures of habit. Plays and novels have for centuries been expected to have heroes and heroines—the selfsame people with whom the twentieth century has been trying to identify. Therefore, in *Coriolanus,* it is disconcerting to find that the central character, the handsomest and bravest fellow around, the center of the sex interest, such as it is—and this we shall discuss later—is really rather horrid. In most plays and stories, the upper-classes are "good," and though there are members of the Good Poor (Cardinal Newman's phrase)— mostly old nurses, coachmen, and retainers of the upper orders —as a whole it is a well-established convention that the lower orders must be either comic or composed of dangerous and undesirable elements. So it is disconcerting in *Coriolanus* to find ourselves unable to identify with either the patricians or the plebeians. No one could say that the Tribunes were Good Poor; neither are they comic. One doesn't know which side to be on.

Today Liberty, Equality and Fraternity are beginning to seem over simple and over esteemed ideas. Now we are beginning to rumble our Tribunes of the People. They are no longer dear little Jack-the-Giant-Killers wrestling on our behalf with the Giant of Capitalism. They are themselves capitalists: rich, powerful, and tyrannical. Furthermore, the figure of Coriolanus, the upper-class militarist, hungry for political power and supported by powerful connections, though still conceivable, has ceased to be a menace. Such a political simpleton, however well-connected with The Establishment, would not last five minutes in modern public life.

And yet, is this true? Coriolanus would have made a fabulous television personality. Handsome as Apollo, a stunning military hero, he would appear, naturally, in uniform, his splendid chest loaded with the glittering testaments of his valor, his brusque no-nonsense manner, his obvious sincerity, the well-known fact of his devotion to wife, baby son and, above all, to his widowed mom. . . . Why, the sheer novelty of a candidate who did not promise to give the voters more of everything they might be likely to want, who did not skate lightly and ambiguously over the thin ice of race equality or religious difference, who did not try to flatter the common man by creating himself anew in the common image, but, on the con-

trary, insisted upon the difference between himself and the
herd and promised only blood, sweat and tears . . . ! A cinch.
The electorate would be knocked flat on its collective back
and vote him a legislative blank check.

So, perhaps, *Coriolanus* may be due to make a comeback
in the theatre, not as the almost clinical examination of the
character whom Shakespeare imagined, but rather as a passionate political affirmation of the public need for an Almighty
Father. A spanking, blockbusting *Heldentenor* could be wafted
to theatrical triumph on the wings of political enthusiasm.
And if you ask how the *Heldentenor* could achieve the deser-
tion to the Volsces and the betrayal of Rome without losing
sympathy, then you do not know anything at all about the
magic of the theatre. Think for a second of Henry V, about
the magic of *Heldentenoren* when they fire off rhetorical tirades
of high caliber, and about the blind gullibility of an audience
in the grip of powerful prejudice.

But none of this has much to do with *Coriolanus* as evi-
denced by Shakespeare's text. Shakespeare was not concerned
to glorify a hero, still less, cheaply, to debunk him—although
he was, I think, concerned to debunk certain upper-class conceptions about honor. He was intending rather to examine
the human being, weak, fallible, like all of us, and, again like
all of us, lost without the love and approval of those whose
approval and love were the sun and moon of his private world.

It is interesting to compare Shakespeare's treatment with
Plutarch's *Life of Coriolanus,* from which he derived the story.
Plutarch allows us to feel that the plebeians have a better case
than Shakespeare grants them. Plutarch's Coriolanus, therefore, appears even more unreasonable and intractable than
Shakespeare's. But, broadly speaking, the political picture is
similar. What Shakespeare has done is to suggest more plausi-
ble and interesting reasons for the shocking treachery of
Coriolanus after he has been banished from Rome. Plutarch
assumes that he was motivated solely by outraged pride. Plu-

tarch, with his strong democratic and liberal bias, implies that Coriolanus's conduct is no more than the reverse of that medal whose obverse is an upper-class, military notion of honor.

Shakespeare, too, takes some pretty shrewd cracks at this kind of honor. Volumnia, particularly, is allowed some scarifying remarks of a kind which are only too familiar in the mouths of elderly females of military caste. Her very first speech whacks home the satiric point, and lets us understand that the fatherless, only son of such a widow had no alternative but to try to be the kind of man his mother had determined to make him. Side by side with Volumnia, Shakespeare places two other figures of great significance in the explanation of Coriolanus: Menenius (a charming humorous aristocrat, an old friend of the family, and a father-figure to Coriolanus) and Tullus Aufidius.

In Plutarch, Aufidius is no more than the protagonist of the Volscian politico-military theme. Shakespeare makes him far more important. As early as the second scene of the play he is introduced for no other purpose than to show him to the audience and to establish from the start that he is an important figure: he is shown dominating a meeting of the Volscian senate. The matter of the debate could easily have been conveyed to the audience in the preceding scene, and indeed most of it is. But Shakspeare considers it important that we should see and hear Aufidius and get an impression of him as one of the dominant elements in his scheme of the play.

He has already been described in the dialogue of the opening scene as the chief military rival of Coriolanus:

> Were half to half the world by th' ears, and he
> Upon my party, I'd revolt, to make
> Only my wars with him: he is a lion
> That I am proud to hunt.

Later, at the start of the battle sequence in and around Corioli (Act I, Scene 4) he is once more planted as the adversary whom

Caius Marcius (not yet created Coriolanus) longs to meet. And again, in Scene 5: "There is the man of my soul's hate, Aufidius." Throughout Scene 6 this theme is repeated, and finally, in Scene 8, the two meet in single combat. This is one of those scenes which an inattentive or inexperienced reader might lightly slip over, since the lines convey no more than the commonplaces of formal defiance. But in a well-ordered production, this is the crisis toward which the preceding sequence has been building.

In Shakespeare, these single combats are always of symbolic importance. Compare, for instance, Hamlet versus Laertes, Macbeth versus Macduff, Richard III versus Richmond. They represent the resolution in action of an antagonism which has already been implied in the dialogue and which is crucial to the whole meaning of the play. Nowadays in the theatre they tend to be skimpy and perfunctory—a few stylized whacks and innocuous bangs. This is all wrong. They are intended, like the great passages of rhetoric, not merely to jet-propel the meaning of the story, but to thrill the audience with a display of virtuosity and, because of that, to be "high-spots," quite apart from their contribution to the plot. In this instance, the single combat is interrupted: *"Certain Volsces come in the aid of Aufidius. Marcius fights till they be driven in breathless."* The interruption serves two purposes: it shows Marcius as a superman, able to cope with a whole group of adversaries, and it plants the eventual assassination at the hands of Aufidius' confederates. This time, Aufidius chides them for their "officious" assistance. (It seems to me a nice point whether or not the actor should be really angry with them or merely accuse them of officiousness for the benefit of bystanders and because their intervention has failed.) Two scenes later, again emphatically placed—a quiet low-keyed scene after a long, rowdy, bustling sequence—Aufidius, in a speech of formidable rhetorical power, voices his passionate hatred of Coriolanus.

Now the play moves on to the political business of creating Coriolanus Consul—business which, though interesting and full of good theatrical effects, does not, as far as I can see, add much to our insight into the principal characters. The rather reasonable objection of the Tribunes to Coriolanus as Consul is his intransigent arrogance, his true-blue, dyed-in-the-wool conservatism. It does not seem to me, any more than it did to the Tribunes, a good idea to appoint a man to high political office just because he is a national hero.

In the fourteenth scene of the play (Act III, Scene 1) the theme of the Volscian war is briefly interpolated into that of the consular election. The defeated Volscians are said to have rallied and to be ready once more to attack Rome. But the threat of war is not taken seriously. Instead, concentration is centered upon the personal antagonism between Coriolanus and Aufidius. Aufidius' remark is reported to Coriolanus, "That of all things upon the earth he [hates] Your person most; that he would pawn his fortunes To hopeless restitution, so he might Be call'd your vanquisher." And Coriolanus wishes he could "oppose his hatred fully."

The play then returns to the business of consular election. The Tribunes forbid Coriolanus to assume office. He rounds on them furiously, refuses to be pacified by his patrician friends and warns them of the dangers of yielding to democracy. The Tribunes put him under public arrest; a scuffle ensues in which the plebeian party is forced to withdraw, and the situation now holds a serious threat of civil war. In the face of this, Menenius promises the Tribunes that he will bring Coriolanus before the people to apologize.

The action then moves into the home of Coriolanus. It is Volumnia, his mother, who finally prevails on him to meet the people, in a long, interesting, psychological scene, the more notable because it is a quiet interim between preceding and subsequent scenes of noisy, agitated bustle. This section of the play comes to its peak with the banishment of Coriolanus, followed by a brief coda, when he bids farewell to his friends at the gates of Rome. The tone is heavily ironical, and the scene ends on his assurance to the family:

> Bid me farewell, and smile. . . .
> While I remain above the ground you shall
> Hear from me still; and never of me aught
> But what is like me formerly.

They hear nothing of him whatever, until he appears before Rome at the head of a Volscian army which threatens to destroy the city and all its people.

The audience, however, now sees Coriolanus, *"in mean apparel, disguised and muffled,"* at Antium, the stronghold of the Volsces, where dwells Aufidius. Now, for the first time in the play (Act IV, Scene 4), Shakespeare makes use of soliloquy —a device which he always uses partly to reveal the real, as opposed to simulated, feelings of a character, and partly for particular emphasis. In this case the soliloquy takes the form of a little meditation, on the part of an otherwise completely unmeditative person, upon the interchangeable nature of love and hate. It is the perfect preparation for what follows—the *scène à faire*, the confrontation of the play's protagonists.

It should be recalled that these two meet three times in the play: their single combat, interrupted by the Volscian supporters of Aufidius, this scene (Scene 5), and the final scene, where, before Coriolanus can defend himself against the furious and jealous accusations of Aufidius, he is butchered by the selfsame Volscian supporters.

The scene which we are now considering cannot be truly regarded as other than a love scene. The soliloquy indicates this: the language and imagery of Aufidius' speech (Act IV, Scene 5, lines 108–141 in the Yale and Oxford Editions) make it unmistakable. Were I to direct the scene, I would suggest that at the end of Coriolanus' speech (line 107) the audience should be unable to tell from the expression of Aufidius what the effect on him of this speech has been. The suspense should be sustained until, after a long pause, he begins to speak very gently and emotionally. Coriolanus should be moved, but not surprised, by this gentleness, but not till the end of the phrase, "I'd not believe them more Than thee, all-noble Marcius" (line 112) should his emotion express itself in tears. He should cry like a child—the pent-up tears which he could not shed before the Romans—and be clasped in the arms of Aufidius like a child by his father. The scene explains the otherwise incredible and shocking treachery of Coriolanus. Shakespeare has rejected Plutarch's simpler explanation, that he simply betrayed Rome out of pique, like a spoiled child.

The spoiled child, the dominating widow's only son, is shown; the inadequacy of the wife and the father-substitute are shown; but side by side with these there has been built up the important figure of the hated rival. Rome—an image of mother—has rejected him; and, be it noted, the rejection was precipitated because, against his better judgment, he yielded to his real mother's advice that he should confront the Tribunes and the people. In his mind, she was responsible for, and therefore guilty of, the brutal rejection. The wounded animal, homeless, has to seek shelter somewhere. The hated/loved rival, the Laertes to his Hamlet, the Macduff to his Macbeth, the Creon to his Oedipus, is sought.

I am aware that I have ventured into the domain of psychoanalysis and I do so with humility. But I think it is clear that Shakespeare is again and again concerned to show that people under great stress act in a grossly unconventional, and apparently illogical, manner, and that the explanation of such action is what his tragedies, and to a considerable extent his comedies, are really about. Those of us whose business it is to prepare his plays for the stage are constantly brought face to face with our inadequacy to interpret the most interesting and mysterious aspects of his work. The scholars have signally failed here. They have wrought nobly to untangle knots which an intelligent application to the *text* can solve. Again and again, however, it is apparent that the text alone is only a limited guide. "Over and above," and "between the lines," not in them, lies the real meaning. Moreover, when it comes to the meaning of a scene, a character, a crucial moment, the scholars take refuge behind a barricade of textual pedantry; a fusilade is fired of cross-references, suggested commas, interpolated colons and dashes, but no attempt is made to capture the fugitive meaning.

What I am trying to say is that, ill-equipped as I know myself to be, I must try to give the psychological explanation as I see it.

Rome and his mother have jointly cast out Coriolanus. The image of the career-rival now presents itself as a possible father or elder brother, something which has always been missing in his life. Hate turns to love—a surprising transition, to make us accept which is the purpose of the soliloquy. In a relationship somewhere between a son and a lover he throws himself on the mercy of Aufidius.

The attitude of the latter is ambiguous. In this scene, he embraces Coriolanus and shows to him a tenderness which is at least fatherly, or brotherly. Later, he becomes jealous, and finally, violently hostile.

Is his attitude in this love scene sincere?

I think so. As with Coriolanus, his protestations of hatred have been suspect in their violence. It is an ambivalent love-hate. In the tenderness and, let us not forget, the surprise of the moment, he embraces Coriolanus in all sincerity and promotes him to a position and power which he afterward, in cold blood, regrets.

The final scenes of the play are of superb and thrilling mastery, but they present no new twists or surprises of character. It should be noted, however, that the chilling and killing rejection by Coriolanus of Menenius' plea to have mercy on Rome corresponds to the classic pattern of the murder of the father-figure by the protagonist—a pattern which Freud found so significant in the Oedipus legend, and which he claimed is repeated to greater or lesser degree in every human life. Menenius is to Coriolanus what Laius is to Oedipus, Duncan to Macbeth, Caesar to Brutus, or Polonius to Hamlet.

Julius Caesar

What is this play about?

The title of a Shakespearean play often offers a key to its meaning. It is surely an odd but significant thing that in this play the part of Julius Caesar, though very effective, is very short. He is killed about half-way through the play, and even while he is still alive he is never the chief character. Clearly, then, it is not about the *life* of Julius Caesar. But, arguably, it is about his *death* and, I suggest, it is about the reasons for his death, the death itself, and then, most importantly, the consequences of his death.

This is a case where the plot, or story, of the play can be clearly differentiated from the theme. By the story I mean the sequence of events which occur to the characters of the play, either before our eyes in action, or else in narration, like Casca's description of the offering of the crown to Caesar. By the theme I mean the idea, or complex of ideas, which is the author's comment upon the story.

Remember that it is not possible, it simply is not possible, to tell even the simplest story without some kind of comment. Such comment need not be conscious. Often it is made when the storyteller, or author, quite unconsciously omits some element, or stresses another, or invents something on the spur of the moment. Such omissions, emphases and inventions give to the story the particular slant which the author requires it to have, usually for reasons of which he is unaware.

In this case, however, comment is very conscious. Let us consider what Shakespeare means to imply by considering very briefly the structure of the play.

The first scenes establish the situation: Caesar is likely to assume absolute power in Rome. A group of aristocrats, for various reasons, feels so strongly opposed to this that each of them is prepared to go to the length of assassinating the

would-be dictator. Of this group the principal figure is Brutus,
a man moved by no personal hostility to Caesar, but only by
consideration of the public good. Brutus, at the beginning of
the play, is uncertain where he stands. He hesitates to upset
the regime, recoils in horror from the act of murder. The
murder-plot is the conception of the clever and ambitious
Cassius, who brings to bear on Brutus every influence he can.
By the end of the fourth scene Brutus has been persuaded to
head the conspiracy.

The assassination takes place.

Then Brutus makes the fatal political mistake of allowing
Antony, a handsome young friend of Caesar, to make the funeral oration over Caesar's body. Antony uses the occasion to
inflame the anger of the Roman populace against the aristocratic
conspirators; Brutus and Cassius are forced to fly from the
city; Antony joins forces with Octavius, Caesar's nephew and
heir. The removal of the dictator has been achieved, but at
the cost of civil war.

At this point we are only about two-thirds of the way
through the play. It is now clear that Brutus, not Julius Caesar,
is the play's central figure. Clear, too, that the play is less concerned with the actual murder than with its consequences.

The remaining scenes show the Caesarian Party, led by
Octavius and Antony, defeating the Conspirators' Party. This
defeat is the more inevitable because of the disaffection between Brutus and Cassius. At the same time we are shown
that all is not well between the victors either: Octavius and
Antony too are at odds.

Side by side with this picture of political and military disintegration is shown the personal disintegration of Brutus.
Like Macbeth, he is a great man, haunted, sapped, and finally
destroyed by the guilt of murder.

In performance, as in so many of Shakespeare's plays, it is
easier to hold an audience in the early and middle parts of the
play than in the last third. This is not, I think, because the author's work deteriorates. The difficulty arises because the final
scenes of Shakespearean tragedy show the conflict resolved in

combat—action of a kind (battles, suicides, violence of all sorts) which cannot be made convincing by the naturalistic methods which have, for some generations, dominated theatrical presentation.

The final impression created by the pell-mell sequence of disasters, culminating in the defeat and death of Brutus and the uneasy triumph of Octavius and Antony, should be one of disintegration, the falling apart of what the whole conspiracy had been designed to protect: the body-politic of Rome.

This is not an easy effect to achieve because, again, it is at odds with customary theatrical procedure. Usually plays are designed so that the end brings all the loose ends of the story together and offers them to the audience tied with a neat bow of silver ribbon—the happy-ever-after convention. Or, where a "happy" ending is quite out of the question—as in *Hamlet*, *Macbeth*, or *King Lear*—the ending shows the tragic events of the play irradiated by the hope of a more auspicious future.

Here, however, the whole point is lost if the future is indicated to be anything but gloomy and confused. Like Sophocles' *Oedipus*, this is a tragedy where the good intentions of the central figure are rewarded with nothing but disaster; at the end, the audience is left to take what consolation it can, not from virtue rewarded and vice punished, but merely from the fact that the chief character has steadfastly done what he *believed* to be right.

This is what I believe to be the conscious comment of the author.

There is a further comment, of which he may also have been conscious, but of which he was more probably only partly aware. It is a hidden theme of many, perhaps most, of his serious plays. Brutus, like Macbeth, murdered a man who stood to him in the relation of king, or father—for a king is a symbolical father, what psychologists call a father-figure. Julius Caesar, like King Duncan, like Hamlet's father, is one more of the great, so-called archetypal figures which haunt the frontiers of human consciousness: the Murdered Father.

Julius Caesar is one of the more popular and frequently

performed of Shakespeare's plays, and very rightly so. In it are endless felicities of expression, moments of insight, exhibitions of those qualities of mind and heart which stamp the author as a master-artist, and those qualities of theatrical workmanship which likewise stamp him as a master-craftsman. His accomplishment in many fields is displayed especially, perhaps, in the scene immediately after Caesar's murder (Act III, Scene 2). The murder itself has been a big scene; whatever follows runs some risk of anti-climax. Shakespeare sets Antony to work upon the Roman populace in a scene which has two of the great rhetorical set-pieces in our language, and which is an absolute model of plot-manipulation. The scene, instead of being itself an anti-climax, makes it very hard to avoid anti-climax in the rest of the play. Indeed, in the theatre I have often known performances to decline from this point on. The only way to guard against this is to find the intention and the pattern, both far from obvious, of the later scenes.

As I have indicated, the intention is to show disintegration, both of the body-politic and of the principal personages of the play. It is expressed in a series of brief, highly condensed episodes, which demand a great deal both from the skill of the performers and from the imagination of the audience. It is easy for the long series of deaths and disasters to seem not only monotonous but a little absurd, especially to audiences accustomed to television and movies. In these media the mechanics and outward appearance of death and violence are treated with respectful realism; whereas the ideas and passions involved—cops versus robbers, good versus bad—are extremely obvious, as a rule, and are treated with contemptuous triviality.

The final scenes of *Julius Caesar* deal with ideas which are neither trivial nor obvious, and in the expression of which realism would be as out of place as a rhetorical, blank verse finale would be in the last ninety seconds of a crime serial. Because the pattern is one to which we are not accustomed, we are apt to express it clumsily, or indeed even to fail to see that it exists.

Visually the powerful Guthrie statement is of course nowhere as eloquent as in the productions he has staged. A representative sampling of these is shown here. [Editor]

OLD VIC COMPANY IN *Hamlet* AT ELSINOR, 1936. LAURENCE OLIVIER AS HAMLET.

OLD VIC COMPANY IN *Hamlet,* 1938. ALEC GUINNESS AS HAMLET.

FESTIVAL THEATRE, STRATFORD, ONTARIO.

STRATFORD (ONTARIO) FESTIVAL COMPANY IN *Oedipus*, 1955.
DOUGLAS CAMPBELL AS OEDIPUS.

STRATFORD (ONTARIO) FESTIVAL COMPANY IN *The Merchant of Venice*, 1955. FRANCES HYLAND AS PORTIA, DONALD HARRON AS BASSANIO.

All's Well That Ends Well, STRATFORD-UPON-AVON (ENGLAND), 1959.

The Matchmaker BY THORNTON WILDER. LONDON 1956, NEW YORK 1957.

The Tenth Man BY PADDY CHAYEFSKY. NEW YORK 1959.

The women's parts are small and comparatively unimportant. I have never been able to find Cato's daughter other than a noble bore, one more instance of the extreme difficulty in making unadulterated goodness acceptable in fiction. Calpurnia's scene with Caesar is far more interesting and unconventional. But her part in the drama is over all too soon.

The fact that in *Julius Caesar* the sex interest is so marginal and so tepid has been, paradoxically, a major factor in the high estimation which the play enjoys in the English-speaking world. In the theatre it is one of the most frequently revived of all Shakespeare's plays and is known to be one of the very soundest at the box-office. It is the play which recurs most frequently in the exam syllabus at every level and in every corner of the educational field. This is because it is a "safe" play for youngsters. Teachers and parents can expose them to it without anxiety about awkward questions or unsuitable giggles or, worse still, the possibility that Horrid Ideas may have been indelibly imprinted upon the impressionable wax of the young mind.

For this reason, *Julius Caesar,* masterpiece though it be, has resulted in so many young people being put off Shakespeare for life that, laid end to end they would stretch . . . the notion is too sad and painful to pursue.

Shakespeare is not a kiddy's playwright. It is no service to Shakespeare, to education or to anything else to expose children to an adult masterpiece before they can possibly be ready for it. *Julius Caesar,* for all that it contains scenes of obviously exciting drama and rabble-rousing popular rhetoric, is a work of highly sophisticated and mature values. The mere absence of sex, even if it were absent, does not make it more understandable by, or more suitable for, the inexperienced young.

The Merchant of Venice

Who is the Merchant of Venice? Shylock's part is the most striking and effective, and he is arguably *a* merchant. However, he is absolutely not a Venetian. I think Shakespeare referred in the title not to Shylock but to Antonio. He is the pivot of the story; his kindness enables Bassanio to woo Portia; to make the loan to Bassanio he puts himself in the power of Shylock; he is an example of gentleness and unselfishness, in striking contrast to all the other principal masculine characters. But even Antonio's gentleness does not extend itself to Shylock, the Jew. Like all the other Venetians in the play, not excluding the Duke at the extremely irregular trial, he shows marked anti-Semitic prejudice.

On this account it has been argued that the play is an anti-Semitic document. But surely, to conclude that the attitude of his Venetians represents Shakespeare's own attitude is as wild as to assume that, because he wrote *Macbeth, Hamlet* or *Richard the Third,* he condoned regicide. The Venetian attitude in this respect is stressed to show the moral climate in which Shylock had to live; it explains, and to a great extent excuses, both his and Jessica's conduct.

Several factors, although his is the title role, combine to put Antonio in the shade. First, Shylock is a much better part—a highly colored portrait in Shakespeare's most exciting vein. Second, the relation between Antonio and Bassanio is not meant to suggest that of uncle and nephew, or just two friends, but that Antonio is in love with the younger man. I will argue this case more fully in a moment, but, granting it temporarily, it is obvious that the idea is expressed between the lines, not baldly and explicitly. In epochs when conventional respectability was of great importance—the nineteenth century, for example—the hint of an "irregular" relationship will have been studiously ignored. Thus this theme will have been omitted from the play and the character of Antonio will therefore have been rendered more simple. He just becomes an entirely uninteresting, "good" man.

The third reason why Antonio, from reading the text, does not seem a very important or interesting character is that in two of the play's important scenes, though he is absolutely central to the meaning of both, he hardly speaks: I refer to the trial scene and the finale.

When you read the trial scene it is the duel between Shylock and Portia that almost exclusively occupies the attention. Gratiano and Bassanio have "moments." The Duke, as the president of the court, must be accorded a certain prominence. But what of the prisoner?

Frequently, even in the theatre, the prisoner passes almost unnoticed. Very often, I think, the set-up and opening moments of the scene are mishandled. The Duke's entrance is importantly arranged, and when he has reached his place he speaks the appointed line: "What, is Antonio here?" Antonio, already in place (and usually a rather inconspicuous place since the most effective acting positions are held in reserve for Shylock and Portia) answers, "Ready, so please your Grace."

I believe that it is not only Shakespeare's intention, but also theatrical common sense, that, since this is Antonio's trial, he should be, if not the principal figure, at least one of the focal points of interest. Shylock and Portia have well-prepared, effective entrances. Common sense dictates this, but it is also apparent from the text.

Antonio, I contend, should also have an important entrance. This is less apparent from the text, but it can very easily be contrived and with no detriment to the entrance of the Duke. The Duke must, of course, have a pompous entrance with procession, fanfare and so on, to the limits of the production's budget. He has to represent the pomp, might, majesty, dominion and power of Venice at the height of her greatness. Besides, the more his entrance is built up, the better by contrast will be that of Antonio, provided that it comes later than that of the Duke. Let the Duke enter with all the theatrical pomp which can be contrived. Let him ask, "What, is Antonio here?" Then let a small and dismal door open from the cells, possibly a trap-door from below, and let Antonio appear between officers—in prison dress, pale, nervous, the very antithesis of the sleek, prosperous merchant we knew before his ruin. Then let him be conducted to a dock, so placed that constantly throughout the scene the focus may be thrown on his reactions to proceedings that are to him literally of vital importance.

The trial scene then becomes an important acting scene for Antonio, and when his turn comes to speak, it is not an interpolation by a half-forgotten personage, but an utterance for which the audience is waiting.

Antonio's speech, when it comes, seems at first glance to be disappointing. It is, to use professional jargon, emphatically "cued-in" by Portia: "You, merchant" ("merchant," note, apropos of the title), "have you anything to say?" One expects a tirade of some kind, a burning self-justification, a thrilling defiance of Shylock, even a monumental farewell like Cardinal Wolsey's in *Henry VIII*. But no. At first glance, and even at second, the speech seems strangely lacking in dramatic impact.

What is the explanation? Did Homer nod? Did Shakespeare try, and fail, to write a movingly eloquent speech? Is the speech —this, I think, is the customary interpretation—a deliberately dull utterance to suggest a dull character? I cannot see what possible advantage Shakespeare could have had in making Antonio a bore. Nor is he so in other parts of the play. Nor, were he intended as a bore, would the play's title be what it is. It would be called *Shylock* or *Portia*—on the analogy that in all the others of Shakespeare's plays that bear the name of a character, the title-part is the central figure.

What then?

I think the significance lies in the fact that Antonio's last words are addressed to Bassanio and in open court. Bassanio is the person who means most to him in the life he is just about to forfeit. He is in no position to pour out intimate, passionate thoughts and feelings. It is a constrained, stiff-upper-lip speech, but nevertheless a final protestation of love, ending with a gallant little attempt at a joke. If an actor playing Antonio keeps this in mind, I believe that the effect can be moving, and the more constrained and embarrassed the manner of delivery, the more moving the speech can be.

I am sure that the intention of the speech is to be moving from the fact that Bassanio's answering protest draws from Portia an "aside" which is undoubtedly meant to make the audience laugh. The theatrical structure is a poignant tension broken by a laugh, and any experienced comedian will confirm that the laugh will come only if the preceding tension has been achieved.

It was consideration of this speech which convinced me that Antonio's relation to Bassanio is what our grandparents called a "tender" one. Granted this, his loan of the money for Bassanio to go to woo the heiress of Belmont becomes much more than the rather easy gesture of a very rich man. And it is ironic that it is his very generosity that brings about his downfall.

Further, it gives infinitely more point to the final scene. Instead of being just a frolic, in verse of incomparable elegance, by the four young people, it is immensely enriched by the presence of the solitary figure of the older man. Not only Bassanio but, on the evidence of the aside in the trial scene, Portia, too, is aware that he loves Bassanio.

I have seen an effectively contrived ending to the play, when the lovers went in to bed, with their jokes and rhymes and laughter still echoing in the garden, where Antonio is left solitary, the papers which confirm the safety of his argosies in his hand. As the lights faded, he slowly let the papers fall at his feet.

Nevertheless, when all is said and done, in the theatre it is almost impossible to make Antonio dominate the play. Although he is the pivot of its plot, and although theoretically it seems to be planned as a conflict between justice and mercy, of which the two protagonists are Shylock and Antonio, it does not work out that way. In the culminating scene of the trial, it is Portia, not Antonio, who is the advocate of mercy; Antonio is relegated to the passive role of Shylock's victim.

It is not generally realized what a long part Portia is. She is in more scenes than any of the other characters and must dominate each scene she plays. I had not realized how important the part was until I directed a production in which Portia was entirely miscast—a sweet, motherly young woman, the epitome of middle-class respectability. The more we stuck her with jewels and decked her up in pink satin, the more she resembled the Railway Queen of some remote junction; the harder she tried to be witty and sophisticated, the more she sounded like a hospital nurse reading a script prepared for somebody else. At the other end of the scale is the star actress who brings a battery of accomplishments to bear and suddenly turns Portia into a wily mantrap, mangling poor Bassanio in her rusty jaws, while, in the trial scene, everyone's sympathy instinctively transfers itself to Shylock as he gets hell beaten out of him by the most formidable female advocate of all time.

The truth is that the part was written for a boy, and exploits both the attributes and the limitations of a gifted boy-player. The companies with which Shakespeare was associated trained youngsters for the stage from a very early age. And the best evidence to their capacity is the fact that Shakespeare was willing to write Viola, Imogen, Rosalind and Portia, knowing that there would be boys fit to interpret them.

The masquerade of Portia and Nerissa in the trial scene really makes sense only when the girls are played by boys. Two boys are no more, and no less, convincing as Doctor and Doctor's Clerk than as Portia and Nerissa; whereas in the modern theatre, two actresses, who seemed credible as Portia and Nerissa, appear at the trial disguised in a manner which makes us feel either that the play has suddenly changed into operetta, or else that the Duke must be a dim old personage indeed not to see that they are a pair of young ladies and have them arrested for contempt of court.

Shylock has been the subject of so much comment and controversy that little more need be added here. It is my view that Shakespeare's portrait is not anti-Semitic, that the pound-of-flesh wager was entered upon as a jest and only turns to venge-

ance after Shylock has been robbed and his daughter ab-
ducted by young Venetians of Antonio's set. In fact, after the
trial, and after Portia's great invocation of mercy, it is the
Christians who lack all mercy toward their enemy. The sadistic
vengeance taken upon Shylock is as offensive to Christianity as
it is legally outrageous. To say this to Jews in the present epoch
is as useless as to beg the rain not to fall. There is a rooted
tradition among Jews that the play is an anti-Semitic document, and it is indeed true that many Jewish boys at school
have, through generations, been taunted and execrated as
"Shylock." This is to the shame of all humanity. But the
remedy is not, I sincerely believe, to boycott Shakespeare's play,
and pretend that it does not exist, but to interpret it so that it
becomes, as its author intended, a fantasia on the twin themes
of mercy and justice, in which none of the characters fully ex-
emplify either, in which none of the characters is either wholly
good or wholly evil, and in which his rightful place is accorded
to the Merchant of Venice.

The Tempest

It is sometimes maintained that Shakespeare's plays are
better appreciated in the seclusion of the study than in the
hurly-burly of the theatre, a point of view arising from a not
unreasonable dissatisfaction with the botched and makeshift
theatrical performances which are too often seen. Without con-
ceding that a stage-play can ever, in principle, be better read
than acted, I must admit that there are certain plays which lend
themselves less readily than others to stage-presentation, and
certain features of plays, otherwise excellently planned for the
stage, which seem to defy presentation.

A reader of *The Tempest* can picture his own enchanted
island, which can be re-created now with the precision of a
well-remembered landscape, now shrouded in a mist of vague-
ness, through which the mind's eye need only decipher such

details as it wishes to see, leaving the rest tactfully obscure. But in the theatre it is not only the island which must be interpreted in tangible terms. Given a good stage-designer that problem need not be insuperable. A far greater difficulty is to realize in terms of flesh and blood the spirits of earth and air and sea which people the island.

I have seen both Ariel and Caliban finely interpreted by imaginative actors; but always, instead of being helped by their costume and make-up, they have had to fight against what had been provided.

There seems to be an inescapable dilemma. If you dress them up with elaborate fantasy, then it is the costumer's fantasy trying to say, in the laborious prose of gauze and wire, spangles and painted cloth, what Shakespeare has already said inimitably. If you shun this horn of the dilemma and attempt an extreme simplicity, you are impaled upon the other horn: the actors have nothing behind which to hide. The simpler their accoutrement the more they are revealed, not as spirits, but as the all-too-human creatures which they are.

Of the two alternatives I prefer the latter. Let Ariel and Caliban appear as what they are—two actors—and let them persuade the audience that they are spirits by the art not of the costumer but of the actor.

Yet how does this square with what we may conjecture to have been Shakespeare's intention?

The Tempest is partly a masque. We have evidence (Inigo Jones' designs, for instance, for masques of a date very little later than the first production of *The Tempest* in 1611) that such entertainments were produced with considerable magnificence. There is much to suggest that *The Tempest* was conceived as an elaborate, spectacular production. Iris, Ceres and Juno will have been presented with elaborate stage effects and sumptuous dresses. Does elaboration in this part of the play permit simplicity elsewhere? I think it does. I think it is clear that Ariel's songs are in quite a different musical style from the set-pieces of the masques. If the music is in two different styles, then there is warrant for the dresses being so too.

What of the banquet and the "quaint device" which, according to the stage directions, causes it to vanish? Appetizing-looking magic banquets and quaint disappearing tricks cannot be very simply contrived.

No one can be dogmatic. My own belief is that the masque at the close of the play can be in quite a different convention from the rest. It is, after all, a set-piece, a play-within-a-play, designed by Prospero to entertain the young lovers and, doubtless, to impress poor Ferdinand with the formidable conjuring ability of his future wife's father. It should offer an elaborate and spectacular finale to *The Tempest,* even though the play has hitherto relied upon that severe economy of means which alone permits an audience to use its imagination creatively.

Ariel and Caliban are never precisely described. Ariel, on the evidence of the name, would seem to be an airy spirit. At the end of the play Prospero says, "My Ariel, chick"; but it would be absurd on this evidence to give to the spirit the likeness of a bird. "Chick" is a term of endearment, no more. The stage-direction which indicates the entrance of Ariel disguised as a Harpy adds, "Claps *his* wings . . .", but in Shakespeare's theatre, where no women appeared, the part will almost certainly have been played by a boy. This stage-direction, therefore, need not imply that Shakespeare conceived his Ariel as being of the male sex, or indeed of any sex.

Caliban is more human and unquestionably male. His mother was a witch, and he feels fleshly longings for Miranda. He smells, and apparently also looks, fishy. On the stage, he is most often presented as a sort of gorilla, covered here and there with bits of material intended to suggest seaweed.

Unquestionably something is lost when the imprecise but marvelous suggestions to the reader's inward eye are exchanged for the too, too solid flesh of stage interpretation. On the other hand, I question whether even the most imaginative reader can ever capture the thrill that a powerful actor can evoke when Caliban cringes sulkily and fearfully before Prospero, or when, after his first taste of liquor, the monster yells for freedom.

Similarly, I doubt whether reading can ever make clear the comment upon the very different freedom and captivity that is implicit in the whole relation between Prospero and Ariel. Just intellectually "appreciating" that this comment exists is not enough. It is a comment which is made by interplay between the two actors, by the exchange of looks and by subtleties of vocal color and of rhythm which can *only* occur when two imaginative actors each react to the suggestions of the other's performance, when they create and feel their scenes *together*.

The relation of Prospero to Ariel is far more subtle and interesting than that of master to slave. Each is enslaved. Prospero is, very consciously, the captive of his responsibilities, his conscience, his human weakness, his mortality. By the end of the play he has abjured his "rough magic"; the staff will be broken and the book drowned. The moment, at the very end of the play, when he bids farewell to Ariel is far, far more than the loosing of a captive bird. It is a death—for both of them.

I cannot doubt but that Shakespeare used Prospero to say something in allegorical form both about himself and, more generally, about the power—and limitations—of the creative artist. It is my view that Shakespeare, by now at the end of his career (though not yet fifty; as contemporary lives go, far from an old man), felt his creative powers to be waning. In Prospero he expressed this awareness, not just in respect to himself, but to all "enchanters." Ariel is the "inspiration" which serves him just so long, then leaves him to fly, like the wind, whithersoever it listeth. Every one of us, whether professional artist or not, is to some limited extent a Prospero. We can all exercise enchantment through the power of inspiration, imagination—call it what you will—fitfully, from time to time, according to our abilities. Sooner or later the moment comes when each of us must break his staff, drown his book, bid farewell to Ariel and accept the fact that "we are such stuff as dreams are made on, and our little life is rounded with a sleep."

On the stage Prospero is presented usually not merely as a godlike figure, which is all right, but as a being of extreme and hoary eld. This is all wrong. On the prosaic level it makes him a rather unlikely papa for Miranda, who is obviously very young. On a deeper level, if Prospero is a venerable graybeard, all passion spent, his relation to all the other characters is emasculated and falsified: his jealousy of Ferdinand, for example, or his passionate resentment of his brother's usurpation and treachery.

The tempest which wrecks the ship, casts his enemies upon the island and places them in his power is a symbol of the rage that is tearing Prospero. It must be a formidable tempest. Unless it is apparent that, right up to a critical moment (in Act V, Scene 1) when he suddenly changes, Prospero really means to exact violent revenge upon the wrongdoers, there is no story. The play would then simply be about a kind old enchanter who had brought about the shipwreck just to give his enemies a bit of a fright—just enough to make the usurper, Antonio, surrender the dukedom. There would be no crisis and no development in the character of Prospero.

But if Prospero is played as a mature but still passionate man, and if in the earlier scenes he is clearly animated by a formidable desire to punish his enemies, several interesting and dramatically valuable things occur. First, the play has a dramatic suspense, which it would otherwise lack: What will happen to the wrongdoers? Second, Prospero's treatment of Caliban becomes consistent with the rest of his conduct. Usually one wonders why such a nice, kind, old buffer is so gruff with the help. Third, the reason is explained why Ariel, as well as Caliban, is eager for freedom. Fourth, and principally, the play has a crisis.

At the end of Act IV the revenge is going great guns. Trinculo, Stephano and Caliban are going to have their joints ground with dry convulsions and several other juicy punish-

ments, not in the least consonant with the nature of kind, sil-
very granddad. As Act V begins (and I think it is obvious that
no break in the action is intended) Prospero moves against the
chief conspirators—and with the utmost relish.

> Now does my project gather to a head;
> My charms crack not, my spirits obey, and Time
> Goes upright with his carriage.

This mood continues until Ariel describes the weeping of the
good, old lord, Gonzago.

> His tears run down his beard like winter's drops
> From eaves of reeds.

That causes Prospero to feel a twinge of compassion. Ariel,
who is Prospero's "inspiration," his contact with the ethereal re-
gions, presses the point:

> Your charm so strongly works 'em
> That if you now beheld them, your affections
> Would become tender.

Prospero's reply is:

> Dost thou think so, spirit?

This could be uttered with grim irony; or it could show the
beginning of the idea of forgiveness. I prefer the former. Then
Ariel utters what, well spoken, can be one of the most touching
and evocative lines in all literature:

> Mine would, sir, were I human.

That is the crisis.
    Prospero replies:

> And mine shall.

He goes on in a marvelous passage to the resolution:

> Though with their high wrongs I am struck to th' quick,
> Yet with my nobler reason 'gainst my fury
> Do I take part: the rarer action is
> In virtue than in vengeance.

Immediately there follows the invocation to the world of nature to witness that henceforth he abjures his rough magic, to
witness the voluntary abdication of the great enchanter.

From this point, relieved by some excellent fun, the play
moves on to its serene close of reconciliation and forgiveness—
dominant dramatic themes of all Shakespeare's later plays—
and the dismissal of Ariel. After the tempest there succeeds a
golden calm.

6. THE WORLD OF
THORNTON WILDER

MY FIRST ENCOUNTER with Thornton Wilder as a man of the theatre was in Glasgow about thirty years ago. I was judging a competition between amateur dramatic societies; a Jewish group offered what I recall as a brilliant performance of *The Long Christmas Dinner*. This short play fascinated me because it discarded a lot of theatrical conventions of which I had become tired (and have since become more tired), notably the pretense of naturalistic illusion.

In *The Long Christmas Dinner* the stage has to have two doors. One symbolizes Birth, an entrance; the other Death, an exit; characters entering the scene are born, they strut their little hour upon the stage and eventually make their exits by a door through which, sooner or later, we all have to pass. The stage, then, represents life. Its only furniture is a long table, spread for Christmas dinner—the feast of life.

That struck me as a great way to present a play. I bought the printed text, liked it as much as the performance, and bought the author's other dramatic work, a book of short plays called *The Angel That Troubled the Waters*. These seemed to me no less interesting, congenial and original than *The Long Christmas Dinner*. Some of them were written to be acted, some of them for what is called the study. Two at least of them still seem to me masterpieces of their kind: *The Happy Journey to Trenton and Camden* and *Pullman Car Hiawatha*. Again they discarded naturalistic illusion in favor of symbolism, a symbolism which is not at all pompous or pretentious, but is, on the contrary, extremely simple and full of a dry, rather Puritan humor.

Yet none of these works could truthfully be regarded as likely to hit the jackpot of popular favor. In thirty years of effort I have persuaded people to let me stage two of them. *Pullman Car Hiawatha* we produced in Liverpool as part of a summer course in drama. In a drill hall or badminton court or skating rink relatives of the cast applauded the single and private performance. *Love and How to Cure It* was presented professionally as a curtain raiser to *Candida*. It had a successful tour and London run and was excellently acted. But I think the public only came to see a mother-goddess film star in the role of Candida.

The next Wilder play I saw was *Our Town*. I had already read and greatly admired the script. Before the commercial production in London it had already been seen in a production by and for GI's which played a limited number of private performances. These I did not see, but they were the object of great local professional respect and admiration.

When the play was finally produced in London by a celebrated American director and a good American cast, it was a failure. Critics damned it and the public stayed away in considerable force. I am convinced that this failure had nothing whatever to do with the quality of the play. Some adverse criticism has been heard of certain aspects of the performance, but my own opinion is that it failed for reasons solely connected with the particular time when it appeared.

The production came just after the end of the war. London had had more than five years of danger, hardship, blackout and all-pervading austerity. What people then craved of the theatre was an escape into a world of prettiness and elegance and luxury. This period was the peak of the ballet mania. The right theatrical recipe was ballerinas in pink, floating in three-four time through pleasures and palaces to a predestined ending of elegant bliss in the arms of A Prince in White Tights.

What Wilder and his collaborators offered were some serious, homely goings-on in front of black drapes; no glamor, and,
to add insult to injury, the goers-on were prosperous, comfy
homebodies, quite untouched by bombings, or blackouts or
food shortages. I shall never forget the drop in the spiritual
temperature, the nipping frost of disapproval, which settled
upon a small but earnest audience, when one of the actresses
in the play bade the milkman to leave three quarts of milk
next morning. We had for some time been limited to half a
pint per person per day. The jealousy was, of course, unreasonable but understandable. The production, in short, hit London
at a bad moment.

Since then I have seen several other productions of *Our
Town* by British companies, which came at a more appropriate
moment and so made up in timeliness for what they lacked in
authentic American dialect and atmosphere. The play has now
established itself, not merely in the English-speaking theatre,
but all over the world, as one of the hottest modern candidates
for classical status.

In *Our Town,* as in his short plays, Wilder substitutes symbolism for naturalism, ritual for illusion, and discards elaborate
scenery for a bare stage. A few chairs and a table or two do
duty for everything that is needed in the play. The actors do
not even have real props. They pretend to be grinding coffee,
drinking an ice cream soda or tacking a straggling creeper to
the wall of a house, with nothing to aid them but their own
skill in mime and the imagination of the audience. It is an
essential part of Wilder's theatrical creed that the theatre is a
place where actors and audience meet in a game—a profoundly
serious game—of make-believe; also that the imagination is best
nourished on a simple diet. For an audience to imagine a room
it is not necessary to erect walls, doors, windows and show a
lot of fancywork in the way of furniture and fittings; to imagine
that the actors are out of doors it is not necessary that they
should appear in front of a heap of junk representing trees and

fields and hills and sky. In some plays it is desirable, but it is not necessary. In Wilder's plays, as in those of Shakespeare, Molière, or nearly any of the great masters, other than those of the nineteenth century, it is not even desirable.

Wilder uses the stage not to imitate nature, but to evoke, with the utmost economy of means, a series of images. He claims that a lot of clutter in the form of scenery and properties and "effects" is a positive hindrance to the process of evocation. This is not to say that plays produced with this kind of economy of means need necessarily look drab and dull. The stage picture can still be interesting and exciting even if it is very simply achieved.

The failure of *Our Town* in London at that particular moment of history does not invalidate the principle of simplicity. Nor does that particular failure invalidate another basic principle of Wilder's writing: he is essentially an American writer, a New England writer, writing about his own environment. Authenticity to this environment is essential if the best results are to be achieved in production. But at the same time his plays are sufficiently true to universal human experience, sufficiently transcend merely local environment and character, to make them acceptable on a cosmopolitan level. I believe that such a close attachment to, and interpretation of, a particular part of the earth is an absolute essential to any work of art which can ever be of deep or lasting significance. It is one of the paradoxes of art that a work can only be universal if it is rooted in a part of its creator which is most privately and particularly himself. Such roots must sprout not only from the people but also the places which have meant most to him in his most impressionable years.

In Wilder's case the heredity was New England. His father was a typical New Englander and typical of his time in his insistence on the Puritan virtues, upon low living and high thinking. Temperance and continence were strictly and constantly enjoined; there was, evidently, a formidable insistence upon "Thou shalt not." It is possible that, as so often happens, this insistence upon the negative side of virtue turned a family of high-spirited youngsters into exceptionally positive people.

During Thornton's youth the family moved from place to place in a manner far more customary in America than in Europe. The father was for a time United States Consul in Hong Kong, then ran a newspaper in Madison, Wisconsin, then in California. But always and everywhere the Wilders were consciously and purposefully an American family, upholding what they believed to be good American customs, standards and beliefs.

Thornton contends that up to the First World War, America was a much more homogeneous society than it is now; it was still predominantly rural, still governed by predominantly rural and Puritan conventions, far less rich and comfortable than now, but also less plagued with the complexities and neuroses that accompany wealth and comfort. The problems of a highly industrialized urban society then applied to only a minority in American society and were not a major factor in the formation of American character, thought, speech and behavior. Consequently, what seems to have been a series of extremely diverse environments and a rather rootless childhood was, he contends, in fact not only typically American but consistent to a single pattern.

It is significant that the father conducted the education of the five remarkable Wilder children according to two dominant principles: they must go, the girls as well as the boys, to schools where they would meet not just children whose economic background was similar to their own, but also children from homes both far richer and far poorer than their own. Also, that during the period of their education each of them should spend at least one year abroad.

Thornton's year abroad took him to Rome and Paris. After that he became a school teacher in the Midwest. In his middle twenties he published *The Bridge of San Luis Rey*. This huge success brought both world-wide acclaim and the financial encouragement to give up teaching and become a writer, to give up a settled life and roam the world.

In the theatre, Wilder followed *Our Town* with *The Skin of Our Teeth*. In this play, the technical method is more of a compromise. It relies more than does *Our Town* upon spectacular effect. In theme, also, it is more elaborate. It is an allegory about human tenacity, the capacity of the human race to survive by the skin of its teeth the various disasters to which flesh is heir.

I like it less than *Our Town* just because it is less simple. The allegory is presented with extraordinary verve and humor. But, in my opinion, the manner rather overwhelms the matter. One admires the dazzling virtuosity, laughs at the jokes, but the emotional aspects of the theme get jostled out of the picture. One cannot see the wood for the trees. All the same, there are some mighty fine trees just bursting with gaudy flowers and rich fruit—some sweet, some bitter, some smooth, and some distinctly prickly.

So far in the theatre it has had a more successful career than *Our Town*. This, I guess, is because it offers more spectacular and effective opportunities for the leading players to shine. But so far neither has been what is called a "smash hit." Professional dramatic critics, being but human, are leery about praising the unorthodox; the public rarely shows enterprise when in search of entertainment. Yet these two plays have quietly earned acceptance the world over among discriminating people as works of importance. Where the discriminating lead, the herd invariably follows. These are likely contenders for survival long, long after scores of money-making comedies, which the critics commended and the public adored, have reached utter and deserved oblivion.

With Wilder "so far" is an important qualification. His work is not to be measured in terms of immediate popularity. One of his early plays was *The Merchant of Yonkers*. This was first produced in New York in 1938 under the direction of the great Max Reinhardt. It failed. Seventeen years later the author rewrote it, retitled it *The Matchmaker* and produced it in London. This time it was a success and the same production opened in New York in 1955.

In *The Matchmaker,* Wilder is apparently aiming at quite another target than in *Our Town* or *The Skin of Our Teeth. The Matchmaker* makes absolutely no attempt to explore new theatrical territory. On the contrary, it is a farce in the most traditional style, making use of many of the familiar devices which have been employed in farce from Aristophanes to *Three Men on a Horse*: mistaken identity, hiding under tables and in cupboards, men dressed up as women, lost purses. Although at a first glance the technique may seem entirely different from that of his other plays, there is one point of essential similarity: there is no attempt to make the audience accept illusion. Just as in *Our Town* and *The Skin of Our Teeth,* so the audience at *The Matchmaker* is not asked to believe itself anywhere but at the theatre.

The author uses the mechanism of the theatre not to create illusion but as a constant reminder that the theatre is a symbol of life. The stage is the world. The characters are not merely themselves, but representatives of humanity. The elaborate and preposterous plot derives not from life, which it only faintly resembles, but from the theatre.

The background of *Our Town* is the bare stage of a theatre during rehearsal, and the action is interpreted to the audience by a commentator who is described as the Stage Manager. In *The Matchmaker* the stage is gaily dressed and lighted up in the style which was familiar to our grandparents; and the comment upon the actors is made by the characters themselves in the form of asides to the audience.

In both plays, and in *The Skin of Our Teeth* as well, there is no attempt to pretend that the goings-on are really taking place, that the audience is anything but a group of people who have assembled, not passively to accept an illusion, but actively to take part in a game of make-believe. This is the assumption behind all Wilder's work in the theatre; and this is what I principally like and admire.

Thornton Wilder the man? A compactly built person in his sixties, he is exceptionally uninterested in his appearance and usually looks as if he had just got off a railway coach in which he had been traveling for a week.

Like most human beings he is composed of such contradictory traits as would make a character in a play or a novel seem wildly unconvincing. He is probably the world's foremost authority on Lope De Vega; he knows more of history than most history professors; he can talk philosophy with philosophers, painting with painters, music with musicians. There seems to be no book which he has not only read but remembered in vivid detail.

Yet he is no secluded bookworm; he is a wildly gregarious old gossip who likes nothing so much as rushing from party to party, from Colorado to Colombo, Stockholm to Buenos Aires, by plane, by train, by boat; from salon to saloon, from ritzy hotels to dockside pubs, talking, talking, talking, talking. His talk is a low-pitched, incredibly rapid toccata with a flurried counterpoint of gesture. The bony rather square hands endlessly squirm and twiddle and poke holes in the air; and what a second ago was gossip and nonsense has suddenly turned into an immensely vivacious lecture on Plato, or Italian opera in the eighteenth century, or the influence of Joyce and Gertrude Stein, for both of whom he has an admiration which is at once passionate and rational. He is as idiotically stage-struck as a school-girl who has just come back from her first matinee; and at the same time can view the whole theatrical melee, including his own work, with a judge's impartiality and Olympian calm.

He has known almost every celebrated author, artist, musician, actor or intellectual of the day; and he enjoys flinging their names into the torrent, the maelstrom, of his conversation: "As Freud said to me in Vienna . . . I told the President of Harvard . . . When I was in Chicago with Texas Guinan . . . The Pope whispered in strict confidence . . . Woollcott and I in Venice . . ."

But this is no snob, and there is a stillness at the center of the maelstrom. At the end of a conversation in which Wilder seems never to have drawn breath, he will have a shrewd and tolerant and comprehensive impression of the interlocutor.

I treasure particularly happy memories of him at Stratford, Ontario, where he has been a sort of Honorary Fellow of the Shakespearean Company, attending rehearsals, buzzing like a bee in the actors' canteen, splashing dye onto costumes for plague-stricken Thebans, sitting up far into the night at parties, cross-legged on the floor among the youngsters of the company, listening to them with grave attention, drawing them out and pumping them full of philosophy, psychology, religion, gossip, jokes and just plain, practical horse-sense.

7. THEATRE
VERSUS TELEVISION

IN COMPARING DRAMA in the theatre to television drama we
must distinguish between current practice and what may be
happening ten or twenty years hence. This, I think, is a far
more significant distinction than any theoretical contrasts between the two media. Theoretically, both are endeavoring to
offer to audiences a "dramatic" experience, to interpret life in
terms of an acted figment. The practical differences between the
two are largely due to technical and administrative conditions
of a strictly temporary nature. The theatre, for instance, is
administratively set up to offer a large number of successive
performances of the same play. And, to take a technical instance,
television drama is greatly dependent upon "intimacy," because long shots are ineffective for story-telling on a small
screen. Neither of these conditions need be permanent. The
theatre will almost certainly be forced to discontinue the practice of long runs because the most intelligent and lively actors
will not for much longer contract themselves to this form of
slavery, if more attractive alternatives are offered by movies or
television. Likewise the TV screen will not for ever be limited
to its present size; in recent years the visual image has already
become considerably larger, clearer, and can even be seen in
color.

I shall attempt neither theoretic nor long-range comparisons
here, but rather consider some of the things which are happening currently. Furthermore, I shall not regard these two dramatic media as enemies—they are not even, in my opinion,

direct competitors for the same trade—but rather suppliers of a similar, but not identical, need, like the raincoat and umbrella trades.

It is no longer arguable, but an established fact, that movies and TV have completely supplanted the so-called legitimate theatre as the mass distributors of drama. The legitimate theatre is too expensive and too troublesome for all but a tiny minority to cultivate as a habit. It may, however, be sensible to reflect that that tiny minority almost certainly exercises an influence on the thoughts and feelings of the community out of all proportion to its numbers. Also, because the legitimate theatre has ceased to be the dominant means of distribution, we must not conclude that it may not still be a dominant source of ideas. I think it is for two reasons.

First, television and movies are still, and probably will be for a long time to come, enormously dependent upon ideas which were evolved in the theatre, before TV and movies were thought of. Tricks of story-telling, of acting, sleight of hand, carpentry, painting, the whole paraphernalia of illusion which, like children, audiences love. Nearly all these tricks are age-old. Many of them were old when Sophocles produced *Oedipus* in Athens two thousand years ago. Then Molière, Shakespeare, and countless long-forgotten minor craftsmen threw in their two cents' worth. Movies and TV are beginning—and they are still at a very primitive stage—to evolve new techniques of reproduction and distribution. But what they reproduce and distribute is not new. Their stories are—and this implies no discredit; stories cannot be otherwise—rehashes of archetypal myths and legends, which are given a gloss of newness by placing them in current contexts, sprinkling them with current expressions and dressing them in current fashions.

Second, not only were these ideas originally evolved in the theatre, their practice can still only be adequately learned in the theatre. There is only one place to learn how to create in an audience the alternating tension and relaxation of drama, to learn what makes a piece of "funny business" funny, as

opposed to merely mechanically skillful, to learn how to make
dull lines sound witty and witty lines sound wise. That place
is on the stage with an audience out front. There a bright person, be he author, actor or just a technician, can learn, often
very painfully and mostly very slowly, a few useful lessons
about how to amuse, bore, frighten, shock, and generally pierce
the guard of that beloved enemy, the public.

Of course, I do not mean to imply that one must serve a
lifetime in the theatre before writing a film script, or saying
a few lines in a TV play. Films and TV are full of talented and
successful people who have never worked before a live audience;
people, moreover, who sincerely believe that their lack of stage
experience is a positive virtue, that had they been on the stage
their talent would be tainted by the whiff of ham. But which
of these people have made any really creative contribution to
the art which they profess? The intelligent and humble ac-
knowledge their debt to their predecessors in theatrical craft,
and admit that if they themselves lack the experience of being
offered up as a living sacrifice to the cannibal audience, it is a
lack and not a credit, since movies and TV are still aimed at
audiences. The conditions of reception are very different. What
will go in a packed vaudeville theatre where the patrons, all
on pleasure bent, are well softened up by various means, not
all of them artistic—some indeed liquid—what will go in such
an atmosphere will not do at all in the parlor where Ma at the
sewing machine and Pa reading the newspaper and the kids
supposedly doing homework are not softened up at all. Nevertheless, they are still, if sometimes almost unrecognizably, human
and subject to the same responses as other humans. The context is considerably different but basically the same laws apply.
In the theatre the house is not always full, nor the audience
invariably receptive; the old pro learns to grapple with all sorts
in wildly different conditions.

I hope it is clear that I do not regard the theatre and television as antagonists. Television, as I see it, is only incidentally
concerned with drama. I think that plays written especially for

television have about as much future as had radio-plays twenty or thirty years ago. The public for them is immense but they are no more than a useful substitute for people who cannot, or will not, make the considerably greater effort to see a play in the theatre. I do not deny that television occasionally offers good, even excellent dramatic programs. Equally, I do not deny that the live theatre often offers ill-considered rubbish; but its average level is higher both in aim and achievement. And, of course, it should be. Its productions cost more, are prepared for longer and it is, compared to TV drama, what a custom-made article is to a mass-produced and mass-distributable article— more costly and designed for a more discriminating public.

When you try to consider television drama, as a whole, the worthy offerings, alas, slide out of sight, sucked down into the morass of trash. This state of affairs will continue for two reasons. First, the supply of top-class work never has, and never will, keep pace with the demand. Television has created a demand for dramatic material unprecedented in history. A gallant attempt is being made to meet that demand; but, inevitably, very little of the enormous output attains a higher standard than popular journalism. Second, there is no reason to suppose that the public wishes a higher standard than it is getting, and every reason to suppose that what most pleases the largest number of people is what can be assimilated with least trouble. Drama of any consequence cannot be assimilated without effort.

We are informed by audience-research organizations of the enormous, the truly awe-inspiring, numbers of people who form the audience for a popular television play. I cannot regard these figures as significant except in a commercial sense. Fifty million people may be tuned in to a program, and there is no evidence whatever to say whether in the long run—not just tomorrow, but over a ten- or twenty-year stretch—it has more or less influence than another program which was heard by no more than a few hundreds. I do find it significant that so few sponsors dare risk several successive performances of the same dramatic program.

It must be perfectly obvious that this would ensure a far higher standard of performance. The reason against repetition can only be that the sponsors believe their audience only to be concerned with the plot of a play, and that once this is known there will be no further interest. I assume that sponsors and their advisers have good reason for this belief. That being so, one can only assume, as they have done, that the TV public, as a whole, is a great, dull, unsophisticated monster for whom theatrical trash, presented with plenty of fanfare, will do. Obviously there are exceptions—tens, maybe hundreds, of thousands could, and would, appreciate better stuff. But when you are thinking in tens of millions so inconsiderable a minority must go to the wall. They must accept the mass-distributed article designed to please the largest number of people. Pleasure, like jam, gets thinner as it is spread over a wider and wider area. If you want *your* taste to be pleased then you must expect to take more trouble, to pay more; and, if this is not possible, then you must be as satisfied as you can with what is distributed to the masses —not for their education or improvement, but to lure them to buy commodities.

Now I suppose there may be a possibility that the live theatre will succumb to the grave economic pressure to which it is being subjected. What then? Would TV drama and the movies collapse for want of trained talent? Not at all. Much of the writing, directing and acting is at present amateurish. Deprived of the leadership of theatrically-trained people it would become more so, and almost nobody would notice. The silver trumpets of Madison Avenue would proclaim the virtues of naïveté and clumsiness in writing; ineptitude in direction would be hailed, as it often is now, as the simplicity of genius; the humph-and-grunt school of acting, where type-cast Know-Nothings exhibit sex-appeal, would consolidate a triumph, which so far has only just eluded it. Would this matter?

I think so. But I guess I am prejudiced, and anyway the general question of "do good taste, expertise, and traditional values matter?" is beyond the scope of this piece.

Is the live theatre likely to collapse? In my view, not at all. Those who foresee its imminent demise in the face of the competition of mass-distributed drama assume that the theatre does not change. Of course the theatre of Scribe, Sardou and Belasco, were that the only theatre, would have collapsed—did collapse—fifty years ago. But the theatre, like its rivals, is not static, but active. It changes all the time. And the more intense the pressure the more dramatically does it change, not only artistically but technically and administratively.

Not all change is for the better; yet in many ways I think our theatre is being changed for the better, and, paradoxically, some of the healthiest changes are being wrought by TV. From TV we are getting a transfusion of new ideas; we are being forced to more flexible ideas about scenery and grouping. We are being —already almost have been—forced out of the dreary rut of society comedy. Most important of all we are getting a transfusion of new talent, not just actors, who if they are technically masters of their trade can move perfectly easily from one medium to another, but writers and directors. Two instances: Paddy Chayefsky and Arthur Penn. These two served their apprenticeship in television. Both were successful, both were dissatisfied with the artistic limitations of television and hoped that the live theatre, though unlikely to be nearly so lucrative, would provide a more satisfactory outlet for their talent and a happier background to their lives.

I think their example is likely to be widely followed; and I think it may well be that, as the scope of its operation narrows and opportunities for aspirants to get the necessary theatrical training become fewer, the theatre will recruit much of its talent from TV.

How does this square with what I have just maintained, namely, that only in front of live audiences can the theatrical profession be learned?

It means that in television young writers and directors can get an opportunity to learn many valuable first lessons. Then, while they are still young enough to be flexible and receptive, they must get out of the studio—as the noisome den where TV programs are cooked up is amusingly named—get away from cameras and microphones and electronic technicians, and, stripped of these aids which are also encumbrances, expose their naked talent to the gaze of the public.

Why should anyone want to do this? Why change to a worse-from a better-paid job, which is also no less highly regarded and, arguably, more influential and socially useful?

The answer is partly contained in what we have already considered: that only in front of live audiences can true professional expertness be learned. It is also concerned with the unsatisfactory nature of TV as it presently is. What, from the point of view of an intelligent and reasonably successful professional, are some of these unsatisfactory features?

First, technical: TV is still at a primitive stage. The screen is small; color is still only at the very beginning; cameras and microphones are still under very imperfect control—their range of reproduction is limited and they need the constant attention of technical experts who are, therefore, indispensable to a dramatic production. The writer and director must therefore start by facing the fact that at present their expression will be limited at every turn by the frustrations of technical inadequacy and dominated to an alarming extent by the wishes of electricians, sound-men and camera men who, in few instances, are equipped with the kind of taste or education to make their views relevant.

The technical development of TV now is, in many ways, analogous to the point of development which the movies had reached in Mary Pickford's heyday. It is good enough for anyone with a grain of sense to see that it has extraordinary possibilities, but all the time one has to make gigantic allowances because it's all so new.

Recently I was concerned with the TV production of a light opera. I am credibly assured that the photography was notably clear and lively, the sound reproduction far, far above the average low-to-medium-fi. Everyone was friendly and kind.

As an elderly novice I was assigned to the care of an extremely able director, who really did all the work. I just sat and marveled at the way he twiddled knobs and twirled buttons and pushed levers and kept his head in the time-consuming and nerve-destroying delays for endless trifling but necessary technical fiddle-faddles. The technicians were efficient, and couldn't have been more jolly and agreeable. So they ought to have been, since every consideration was subordinated to getting things right for *them*. The actors went back and back, over and over their performances, were pushed here to make room for a camera, nudged there to accommodate a light, fidgeted hither and yon—not to express better their own or their author's ideas, but the better to cover up the fact that microphone and camera are still only rude and primitive transmitters.

In the end we got a no worse than average picture of tiny gray worms wriggling about on a rectangular gray dunghill. They were just recognizable as moving photographs of actors pretending to be sailors on board ship. At one point it seemed to me that the heroine's face, as she sang a love song, appeared to be reflected in the convex side of a shining kettle; at another, three of the sailors—three handsome well-proportioned men—appeared to have the legs of nine-year-old boys attached to normal-sized bodies. My timid question about what I absurdly called distortion was brushed good-humoredly aside by the Big Brother in charge of the controls. "What you think you see," he said, "is the eye of the camera correcting the distortion of mere human vision."

Second, there are the administrative frustrations. I think the worst of these is the obsession with time. So long as time is sold in chunks to Sponsors it will continue to dominate all other considerations in the studio. The whole set-up in the United States, and indeed in most parts of the world, depends upon the fact that Consolidated Midwest has bought the air from nine to ten, and at ten precisely it belongs to United Toiletries. The program, therefore, must run precisely for a given number of minutes, no more and no less. Men, whose stomachs are strewn with ulcers as thick as leaves in Vallombrosa, stand chalk-white, stop-watch in hand, on guard in the studio, charged with the single responsibility of seeing that *Othello* or Beethoven's *Eroica* does not run one tenth of a second over, or under, the time which has been allotted to Armpit Deodorants. The smallest bit-player, the lowliest fiddler at a back desk, must say his single line, scrape his little semi-quaver, with one eye, and more than half his attention, on the clock.

I have no first-hand experience of the vagaries of Sponsors, and I daresay the newspapers, my sole source of information, are no kinder or more accurate about TV sponsors than about politicians or film stars. But it does seem only reasonable that, if Midwest Consolidated has spent three emperors' ransoms on buying an hour of what is called network time—a significantly mixed metaphor—the Board of Midwest Consolidated will want a considerable say in the program, and only natural that the President of MidCon will be considerably influenced by the criticisms of his adored nine-year-old girl. And then, further, maybe it's just conceivable that the viewpoint of a nine-year-old girl, and the Consolidated Midwestern viewpoint of what will sell its product, may not always coincide with what Paddy Chayefsky or Arthur Penn would feel inclined to express.

The fact, however, remains that all these drawbacks are not endemic to TV, they are shortcomings which can, and surely will, gradually disappear if the public becomes sufficiently mature to think the artistic content of a program more important than advertisement and to think of TV as a distributive agent of ideas, rather than of commodities. Also the mechanical problems are gradually being overcome—cameras and sound equipment are improving and a race of technicians is gradually being evolved who can not only look after the machinery but also have an intelligent grasp of the artistic issues involved.

It is heartening to consider what has happened in the analogous field of recorded music.

Fifty or sixty years ago there was already a considerable

public demand for recorded music. But, partly because the demand was relatively unsophisticated, partly because recording was a much more elaborate, expensive and chancy process than it is today, there was very little supply of anything but the most popular and obviously salable works recorded by the biggest names.

Gradually demand has become not merely larger but far more discriminating, and at the same time the apparatus of recording has become both far more accurate and far more accessible. The result is that, in addition to the "pop" market, where a hit record may quickly sell a million discs and almost as quickly lapse into total oblivion, there exists an enormous and steady market for the great classical works, in which new performances are compared with older ones, with the result that there begins to exist a more widespread knowledge both of the works and a more intelligent criticism of performance than has ever been possible before. Further, though the field is far more restricted and offers neither so large nor so fast a return on the financial investment, it begins to be commercially possible to record performances of recondite works for which there can never be a mass demand, by performers who are not in the big-name category, but may nevertheless be musicians of the first quality.

It is possible now to foresee in a not too distant future, that excellent performances will be publicly available through libraries, not only of almost any serious musical work, whether classic or contemporary, but of the poetry, literature and drama of the whole world. It is hard not to believe that, in the fullness of time, a similar state of affairs will exist in respect to television.

Then, just as I begin to cheer myself with this thought, I remember the movies. Movies were just beginning to grow up—not perhaps in Hollywood, which has always been geared to commercial rather than artistic standards and where quick profits have always been greatly preferred to maturity—in Russia and Germany, and to a lesser extent in France and Britain. These were the great days of U.F.A. films in Germany, and, in Russia, Sergei Eisenstein was making the only movies which can begin to compare, in seriousness of conception and elegance of structure, with classical works in other media— *The General Line*, *The Battleship Potemkin* and *Ivan the Terrible*. Then—wasn't it in 1927?—talkies arrived. And it wasn't just John Gilbert and Vilma Banky who went out of business. Suddenly the whole technique of movie-making had to be revised; a whole new range of possibilities was opened up and, simultaneously, a whole new set of problems. For a while, the result was not artistic progress but retrogression.

In my view, though the talkies have raised the average standard of movies, they have never achieved so high a standard as the best silent films. Nevertheless, by degrees the talkies were just beginning to develop content and maturity to match the technical advance of sound, when along came color. A big technical stride forward is once again achieved at the expense of content. Now just as we are beginning to master the additional artistic problems imposed in the studio by the time-consuming and nerve-racking complexities of color-photography, we find ourselves at the dawn of yet another technical discovery—Cinerama. And so it goes on.

Will it be the same with television? Undoubtedly. Color is already with us with its added demands on lighting technique. Then the screen will get bigger. Then perhaps it will be three dimensional. Always in our technological age we may expect the technicians to move ahead of the ideas which the techniques theoretically only exist to express. So far television drama has been most successful when intimately realistic, when it presents a slice of life truthfully, humorously observed and transcribed by a Chayefsky, directed and acted with "groupy" attention to psychological realism, when it does not make any attempt to be larger and more high-colored than the everyday life of very ordinary people. That is humble and sensible and takes realistic cognizance of the fact that at present only close-ups are really effective in conveying an actor's meaning, or indeed in transmitting anything but a very vague and unsatisfactory impression; also that microphones are flattering to low whispery tones and endow them with added significance, whereas loud declamation, when not actually distorted into unintelligibility, is apt to sound frightfully boring and empty.

At the same time it should be remembered that all the drama which has survived from past ages has done so not because it presented a modest slice of very ordinary life, but because, on the contrary, it offers an enormous helping of something larger, louder and more high-colored than most of us are ever likely to experience. Great acting has never been known as such because it is typical of the behavior of very ordinary people. Great acting has always been outrageous. Let television actors aim to to be human, life-sized and natural: great actors never have been and never will be that. They aim to be superhuman: twice as large as life and three times as natural.

It seems to me that a medium which cannot accommodate great acting has no theatrical future. But perhaps it may not be long before microphones and cameras transmit more kindly than at present sights and sounds on a heroic scale.

The principal enemy of television drama is not the temporary inadequacy of the technical equipment; rather it is the fact that in this medium drama will always be overshadowed by the almost boundless potentiality of television as a *recorder of real events*. This means, I believe, that most practitioners who really are interested in the development of television as a means of communication will concern themselves with the presentation of real events; whereas those who are primarily interested in drama will use TV as a matter of convenience and as a springboard into the theatre.

As yet we are only on the threshold of discovering what "actuality" television can do. Except for great events, upon which exceptional efforts and expenditure have been lavished, most of the television news coverage is still but an impromptu expansion of what radio and newspapers have been doing for years. Now and again a great effort is made: I saw the TV coverage of the coronation of Queen Elizabeth II, and also the installation of Pope John XXIII. Both were historical records of abiding value as well as being superb entertainment. I dare say that, by the standards of fifty years hence, both may seem pretty crude pieces of photography, recording and montage. But it is also possible that, as with mid-nineteenth-century photographs and very early phonograph records, the very simplicity and crudity of the technical means will enhance rather than detract from the significance of what is seen and heard.

Then, the debates between presidential candidates Kennedy and Nixon reminded us, not only how vividly television can be applied to current events, but also how it can confuse actuality with drama, highlighting the dramatic aspects of real and often very serious events in quite a frivolous way. It is now difficult to prevent showmanship and theatricality of the most vulgar kind from permeating events where solemnity or, at all events, dignity, would be more in place. The candidates' debates, through no fault of the principal performers, became a personality contest. The excerpts a few years ago from the proceedings of the House Un-American Activities Committee became a drama in which, according to your point of view, you cast Senator McCarthy as an almost unbelievably exaggerated Heavy, or else as the near-saintly Defender of American and Christian civilization. Reality rather easily turns into drama— and not always of the most sophisticated or respectable kind. One of the paradoxical results of this is that, by contrast, a serious and tasteful production of, let us say, *Hamlet* or *King Lear* has more dignity and nobility, and a good deal less hammy theatricality, than a royal funeral, a Congress of Prelates or a debate at the Summit.

What future has comedy in a medium which can so exquisitely satirize the vulgarity and dullness which underlie the glitter of great occasions, so mercilessly expose the ineptitude of great persons? When we have seen in close-up the comedy and pathos of a real Cardinal, who finds that on a great occasion in a real cathedral he has forgotten his glasses or his handkerchief, does it not a little blunt our appetite for the niceties of fictitious comedy? When, so marvelous is science, we can sit any evening in the living room and enjoy a close-up view of mangled bodies being dug out of the ruins caused by an earthquake, bloated bodies being fished out of a flooded river, charred bodies being raked out of the ashes of a fire, epidemics here, explosions there, mine disasters, boating fatalities, gun accidents, teen-age suicides, does all this a little blunt our appetite for melodrama? Or is Shakespeare right when he says that the appetite grows by what it feeds on? Maybe it does. Maybe our hunger for great occasions, with their satiric undertones, for sensation and violence with their implications of the cheapness of life, will only become greater the more we see. That does not mean that such a hunger will be alleviated by dramatic figments of great occasions and great disasters. The more dramatic television makes the presentation of actuality, the more necessary it will be for legitimate drama to escape from actuality, to present not just an imitation of actuality in life-sized, natural terms, but to go back to the Greek and Elizabethan idea of drama—a re-enactment of great stories in such a way that they do not resemble life but rather ennoble and illuminate it, by showing it, not as a series of events connected only by an all-embracing triviality (where Cardinals forget their glasses and ordinary decent folk are paramount and survive cosily in spite of teen-age suicides and mine disasters), but rather as a process where great and mysterious forces grind decent, ordinary folk to pulp, where triviality is not glorified but mocked, and no one, not even Oedipus, Prometheus, Hamlet or Lear, lives happily ever after.

Then there is this to remember: actuality is a series of events presented in chronological sequence and without comment—or, possibly, in the case of TV news, with a necessarily hasty and superficial comment in the most easily apprehensible terms. Drama offers a series of events which have been carefully selected and arranged by an author to form a significant pattern; in the case of great drama, this pattern provides the comment of a great mind.

Naturally this does not mean that drama is more important than real life. To apprehend great drama is arguably more important, and certainly more troublesome, than to apprehend a series of trivial occurrences from real life. The apprehension of drama is an experience of a similar kind to the apprehension of reality; but whether better or worse is for each of us to judge; and the judgment must considerably depend upon the quality both of the drama and the real events which are concerned.

Then as to the acting: when every politician is taking lessons in make-up, every ecclesiastic practicing saintly faces before the looking glass so as to project the Right Image on TV; when royalty, presidents and multi-millionaries bone up on folksy ways and nice homely expressions so as to woo the common man by creating themselves anew in his image, when everyone, literally everyone, believes that by adding a cubit to his stature (easy: you just stand on a box in front of the camera) he can become a television personality—what, you may ask, is a poor actor to do? If he has a real talent for acting and takes enough trouble to develop a technique, there will always be a demand for an actor's services. But not in TV; in the theatre. More and more television acting will be reserved for the amateurs—Queens being crowned, Cardinals losing their specs and politicians wooing the electorate in Nebraska.

8. THEATRE AND THE UNIVERSITY

I USED TO THINK that drama or theatre had no place in a university curriculum, that universities should be concerned with intellectual, not technical, matters, and that drama, like cooking or carpentry, belonged rather to the trade school than to seats of higher learning.

But the divorce between theory and practice, between academic and technical matters, does not seem so absolute as I once supposed—as in British universities it is still customary to maintain. The notion that technical matters are a little beneath the dignity of a good university's attention derives, I suspect, from the idea that manual work is inferior to intellectual. Possibly at extreme ends of the scale this is true; possibly the work of a ditch-digger is inferior to that of a judge or an archbishop. Possibly. But who will say that the manual labor of a surgeon is inferior to the intellectual labor of an advertising copywriter?

Nowadays we are all agreed that surgery, although manual work, requires not merely extraordinary manual skill; the skill must be backed by intellectual knowledge of a high order. But less than two centuries ago surgery was customarily entrusted to the barber. The manual work of surgical operations was divorced from the brain work of the physician. The physician "directed" the work of less highly educated, less highly paid, and less highly regarded persons—the apothecary and "chirurgeon."

Over the years crafts other than that of the surgeon have

gained in status: engineers, industrial designers or farmers, for instance, are no longer regarded simply as workmen. It is recognized that most trades demand a great deal more than mere manual skill. Also, and largely because of this, there is a general trend toward the blurring of social distinctions between different kinds of workers. It is no longer considered vulgar to be engaged in commerce. But certainly in Europe, and more so in America than most people care to admit, it is still considered somewhat vulgar to be engaged in manual work. The surgeon, the engineer, the pianist and the farmer like to be regarded as "professional" men rather than "tradesmen," to stress the intellectual or nervous demands which their job makes rather than its demand for strength and dexterity.

Thus, even in American universities, far more socially egalitarian and far more oriented toward the acquisition of practical skills and "useful" knowledge than the older universities of Europe, there is still a tendency to feel a little ashamed of the more obviously practical aspects of the curriculum and to stress the more purely intellectual. Largely this is an attempt to check the tendency—and it *is* a deplorable one—for a university degree to be regarded as a passport to a better job at a better salary. But is such a tendency wisely checked by insisting upon the intellectual and abstract aspects of subjects which make very little sense if deprived of practical application?

The necessity for learning the relevant practical skills is fully recognized, for instance, in medicine and dentistry; in the sphere of art it is, in my experience of American universities, only recognized to a limited degree and, I suspect, reluctantly. Departments of Drama and Departments of Music concentrate their attention upon the theory and history of their respective arts; they do not entirely omit the practice, but they do not aim to turn out professional practitioners.

Why not? When I asked a professor at a well known American university with a large Drama Department how many of his students had graduated in the last ten years to the professional theatre, the answer, accompanied by a furious glitter of rimless glasses, was "One. Thank God!" Why only one? And why did he thank God?

Recently I spent six weeks in the highly enlightened and liberal Drama Department of another university. Here the faculty believed strongly that drama could not reasonably be taught without mixing practical with theoretic work. Yet even here the technical work was to my mind distinctly sketchy. Drama students were spending a great deal of time rehearsing and performing plays, but most of the performances and rehearsals, which I saw, were of unimpressive standard because neither directors nor actors had, or so it seemed to me, quite adequate technical know-how. They were attempting rhetorical plays—Shakespeare and Greek tragedy, for example—with no rhetorical equipment, no views about rhetoric beyond the conventional American attitude that speaking must be "natural," that the ultimate in rhetorical sin was to "elocute."

The department had no speech teacher. There were classes, and very good ones, in singing; but these occupied but one hour a week in which hardly any individual attention could be given to any single student by the singing-master, who was not a member of the dramatic faculty but was on loan from the music department. There were endless classes and discussions and demonstrations of something called "Dramatic Interpretation." But I fail to see how a student who knows almost nothing about voice-production, diction or phonetics can interpret satisfactorily anything which makes more than the most perfunctory technical demands. No one expects a pianist to "interpret" a sonata of Beethoven or a fugue of Bach, if technically he has not graduated beyond picking out the melody of "Yankee Doodle" with one finger.

A dominant influence of recent years on academic, as upon professional, theatre has been that of Stanislavsky. Now Stanislavsky's theoretic writings are frequently self-contradictory; like any other sensible and lively person he changed his views considerably at different times of his life. Quite apart from this,

I think, in America he has been taken as the great apostle of intuition divorced from technique in acting. While some of his writing certainly does stress the importance of intuition in acting, and does suggest ways of encouraging and disciplining the actor's intuition, I think this aspect of his work has been seized upon and misinterpreted as implying that technique is unimportant.

The reason for this is partly that, in a highly "naturalistic" period in the theatre, the techniques of old-fashioned elocutionists inevitably fell into great disfavor. No doubt there were many terrible elocution teachers and terrible elocutionists. But the tendency of the revolutionaries was, as always, to tip out the baby with the bath water. The existence of bad elocution teachers does not justify the present-day tendency to write off all speech-teaching as an old-fashioned, pear-shaped bore. Nor does it justify the current toleration of a great deal of sloppy, vulgar ignorance about voice-production, and the articulation, pronunciation and phrasing of the English language.

However under the, no doubt sincere, belief that the great Stanislavsky thought inspiration important and technique unimportant, it has become customary to pay almost no attention whatever to the technique of speech in the theatre. In universities this accorded comfortably with "Liberal Arts" philosophy that drama students should be encouraged towards theoretic principles and away from technical practice, should not be encouraged to regard their studies "vocationally."

The Drama Department, with which I have recently been connected, had good classes on the history and theory of drama— I felt the students would have welcomed their being a bit stiffer and harder, but nonetheless there was excellent stuff available. But the pracical side of the work seemed to me too "inspirational." There wasn't nearly enough of what a pianist gets from the deadly but essential scales, arpeggios and Czerny, what a soldier gets on the barrack square.

Part of the difficulty with this particular department—and I suspect that this applies to many departments in many seats of learning all over the world—is indecision about its aim. Is the object of the department to create an interest, rather than an expertise, in drama? Is it to equip students for a career as teachers of drama at other universities or in high schools? Is it to equip them as—fearsome title—Recreation Directors?

This particular department was faced with a rather peculiar element in its graduate classes: a considerable number of graduate students had been attracted from many parts of the United States in the hope of winning one of a limited number of Fellowships, which would enable them to work for a year in a professional theatre. These young people were perfectly clear about their aim: they wanted to equip themselves as best they could for the Fellowship. As the Artistic Director of the professional theatre involved, I, too, was rather clear about what I wanted them to learn: to speak better. I am not of the opinion that the most important aspect of acting is technical. Technique is less important than imagination. Imagination cannot be taught, but it can to a great extent be set free of inhibitions. One of the major inhibitions of American actors is self-consciousness due to real, or supposed, inadequacies of speech.

Unfortunately there are very few good vocal teachers, and very little general agreement exists about what constitutes good teaching or, more fundamental, what constitutes good speech. Until some sensible standards are set and some reasonable criteria agreed upon, the present chaos will continue. Such an agreement must be reached, first of all, inside Drama Departments and inside the limited number of theatres which demand a high standard of speech from their actors. Only slowly will such an agreement spread outward into wider circles of society.

Meantime, until Drama Departments can raise their technical sights, they will continue to turn out young persons, stuffed to the eyes with theory, who are ill-qualified to do much more than impart these theories to another generation of students. The almost total divorce between the academic and professional theatres will remain unreconciled.

This is a pity. Right now the professional theatre could do

nicely with infusions of more educated blood, and the academic theatre would be all the better if its leaders could have tested their theories, and themselves, in the fires of professional experience.

I realize that the most successful and highly equipped professionals may not be anxious to spend a good part of their best energies and best years as teachers. But I wonder whether the universities have really tried to woo them? Whether there has been a sufficiently serious attempt to create the sort of working conditions which might attract them and to recognize the possible value of their contribution?

I should have thought it reasonable that different universities should have different aims for their Drama Departments. Some will prefer to concentrate on theory and these will be staffed by scholars and attract the sort of students who want to be scholars and teachers. Others might prefer to emphasize the practical side and come near to offering a trade-school training. In that case the faculty should have a high degree of practical competence and experience.

One would hope that even the most scholarly department would not wholly overlook the practice as well as theory of dramatic art; and that, vice versa, even the most strictly practical department, deliberately aiming to train professionals, would insist upon a standard of scholarship not inferior to that demanded by such courses as Social Science or Business Administration.

Even the most practical university training ought, it seems to me, to be directed towards imparting a certain philosophy of drama. By that I mean the study of such questions as the following: What is drama? Why has drama from primitive times to that of our own day been a dominant means of human expression? What is a theatre? What is acting? Since only a small part of ordinary social intercourse is completely "natural" are the unnatural assumptions which comprise everybody's social façade to be described as "acting"? What are the social or political or economic or ethical functions of drama?

Intelligent answers to any of these questions must, I suggest, reveal that drama—in a wide sense, not just professional theatre —plays a fundamentally important part in the life of our community and that of every other since, as savages, we danced to make the crops jump from the ground in sympathetic imitation of our action, or smeared our faces with paint and gave terrible cries to make our savage neighbors afraid of us.

Deeper than that, drama is a fundamental element in the private, spiritual life of every one of us. It is expressed in the form of ritual, from the highly conscious rituals of religion through the semi-conscious daily rituals of doffing hats, shaking hands, and so on, to the rituals of which we are so little conscious that they seem only to be habits—brushing the hair or teeth, shaving, or the needful and highly stylized routines of eating and other body functions.

To give intelligent answers would demand a course of studies by no means frivolous, involving, as it would, some acquaintance with aesthetic philosophy, anthropology and psychology, and including the detailed study of theatre history, and research into bygone forms of theatrical architecture and production. The practical value of such answers will depend upon the importance in which drama is held. If the answers reveal what I think they would, then it should be very important indeed. At present we are simply fooling around with this primitive and powerful means of expression. We have, largely, through lack of a philosophy of drama, effected its arbitrary and unnatural divorce from religion, and from most of the more serious sides of both our private and public lives. We sell it for money and rarely value it more highly than as a frivolous pastime, principally devoted to erotic titillation.

As a result of this public attitude toward it, the art of the theatre has become very seriously vulgarized. There is no clear distinction between what is offered as a serious expression of thought and feeling, and what is offered solely as a diversion, and to make money. The professional critics judge both with a precisely similar mixture of good-humored condescension, combined with a knowing tipster's attitude to those who may be about to buy tickets. We in the profession are vulgarly anxious about "success," which means popularity at the box-office. This is excusable because without a certain measure of success we do not eat; but it is insufficiently recognized that popular success and artistic merit are poles apart. Further, the greed for success means that more important aims are neglected. Few of us have time or energy to inquire seriously why we are doing what we are doing, or, indeed, what we are really doing.

Perhaps, then, an important function for a university, in relation to drama, is to suggest a theory of drama. We want from the universities a theoretic, philosophic basis to which practical activity can be related. I do not think in the theatre we need to fear that an established dogma will impair originality of thought or action. In a profession, which places the highest premium upon idiosyncrasy, there will always be heretics.

Some universities will be more, some less, concerned with practice. The more practical departments must, in my opinion, demand higher standards of technical accomplishment. The problem cannot be solved by professorial direction of student-actors. Amateur practice is not the right complement to theory of the weight which should adequately represent a university's point of view. The study of drama could, and should, be more closely linked with professional practice.

This will not be easy. Many Drama Departments exist in colleges which are hundreds of miles from contact with any theatrical activity which could reasonably be regarded as a pace-setter. It is hard for such departments to maintain a sense of standard. Hard, but not impossible. I suggest that the standard of competence in a small, remote medical center does not differ so enormously from that of Johns Hopkins or the Mayo Clinic as does the standard of dramatic production in some small, remote universities from that of a tip-top professional theatre.

This, I suggest, is largely because at any medical center the teaching and demonstration are not just academic matters. The students are constantly under the instruction of the best professional practitioners in the district. Admittedly, competent medical men are far more widely available than competent theatrical professionals, who are almost all centered on Broadway. But demand creates supply. Every small, provincial university will not command the services of Elia Kazan or Franco Zeffirelli in its Drama Department. But I believe that a supply of talented professional men could soon be created, if Drama Departments demanded the same degree of technical competence from their staffs as do hospitals.

Admitted that it is a traditional matter of honor in the medical profession for the best men to make available a part of their time and energies for teaching. I believe that a similar tradition would not be hard to create in the theatre; seniors would be proud and honored to place their professional experience and skill at the service of the younger people who will succeed them.

I am aware that a great deal of what I have been discussing and most of the suggestions I have made have already been discussed and suggested in many universities. Changes are being made, even larger changes contemplated. More and more, I believe and hope, the academic and professional theatres are beginning to be aware that they could be very useful to one another. Experiments in cooperation are already being made. Ways are being sought, still perhaps rather tentatively and timidly, on the part of both sides. The pros are still apt to feel that work with students is a little beneath their professional dignity, and is a virtual admission of professional failure. This is snobbery of a ludicrous kind.

Meantime, in the universities too often the theatrically blind are leading the blind. Ladies and gentlemen with splendid academic qualifications are endeavoring in place of theatrical know-how to substitute erudition, together with earnest and sincere good will toward their students and their task. This is tolerated because the public regards Drama with a big D as a pretentious bore. The theatre to them is fun, and Drama Departments exist to impart a little cultural gloss to more serious studies. Consequently Drama Departments occupy only a very lowly place in the academic hierarchy. I even know universities where the Drama Department is only tolerated if it pays its way. So the professors have to put on the Broadway musicals of yesteryear in order to fill the house and earn their keep. Student performances of *Paint Your Wagon* or *Sing Out Sweet Land* are well in order if they are simply got up for fun or a spare-time activity. But to admit them as part of the curriculum at university level seems to me altogether too low an aim, and to discredit the whole notion of drama as a serious, even respectable, object of study.

Until Drama Departments propose for themselves more clear-cut and consistent aims and give evidence of higher standards of accomplishment, they will not be taken more seriously by Boards of Regents or by students, and they will not attract the professional cooperation, which I believe they badly need.

9. A PORTRAIT

AND TWO PROFILES

Lilian Baylis

Lilian Baylis, though not its founder, was the chief force behind the development of the Old Vic in London, and was the founder and inspiration of Sadler's Wells, with its opera and ballet. She succeeded in making a considerable section of the British public aware that drama, opera and ballet were something more than luxurious toys, and in impressing upon a considerable number of British theatrical managers the idea that there was something more to their job than just the sale of commodities. I do not think it is too much to say that the influence which she exercised on the British theatre over the last sixty years has been greater than that of any other one person.

What kind of woman was she?

I did not know her till quite near the end of her life (she died in 1937), when she was already past sixty and her physical vigor had begun to decline, and by then she was a legendary figure. There were awesome stories of her energy, her storms of anger—more terrible than those of Elijah—her indomitable physical and moral courage, her persistence in the face of adversity, her ceaseless championship of the underdog. There were also the funny stories, which mostly concerned the naïveté which was the obverse of her greatness, her simple-hearted remarks to royalty—to Queen Mary, for example, at the end of a matinee: "Hurry home, dear, you've got to give the King his tea"—or jokes about her chumminess with Almighty God—an actor burst unexpectedly into her office to find her on her knees: "God dear," he overheard, "do send an actor to play *Henry the Fifth*—cheap."

She was a rather short, stout person with glasses. I do not think that she can ever have been a pretty woman, but a slight stroke—the result of a swimming accident—had left her mouth a little twisted and one eye squinted a bit. But you must not think that this gave her a repellant or unpleasant appearance. Far from it, her appearance was extremely endearing. But it was cosy rather than glamorous, odd rather than elegant. Her voice, very strong and rich, was obviously the expression of a highly-charged, powerful person. The accent was far from aristocratic and her vocabulary was peppered with rather out-of-date, schoolboyish slang—"old bounder," "dirty little rotter," "a swizz," or " a priceless lark." In spite of being sincerely and deeply religious she swore a great deal: "Damn" or "Blast" meant nothing; "bloody" little more. And I am told that, when younger, when transported by one of her rages, the language became truly extraordinary—drunken fishporters yelling at their whores sounded by comparison like Little Lord Fauntleroy prattling to Dearest. I suspect that this language had been picked up in Johannesburg, where as a girl she taught music and dancing to the gold miners, and from whence she had been invited by her Aunt Emma to return to London for a while.

Here briefly we must digress to introduce her aunt—Miss Emma Cons, a person very different from, but no less remarkable than, her remarkable niece. Miss Cons was born in 1838 and studied as an artist, or rather, I think, what we should now describe as a craftswoman. She had been, by turns, a metal engraver, an illuminator and a designer of stained glass. During this period (late eighteen-fifties and early sixties) there was a growing movement which was to influence her life. An effort was being made to ameliorate the poverty and squalor of the London slums. Areas of slum property were bought by philanthropists and put into order for the benefit of the tenants. John Ruskin, who had known Emma Cons as an art student, bought some dilapidated property and installed Miss Cons as a part-time assistant manager.

Gradually her social work superseded her work as a craftswoman. Soon, with the help of a group of wealthy friends—she evidently always had an extraordinary gift for interesting rich and important people in her projects—she bought a considerable area of slum property in Lambeth. With a Board of distinguished and titled persons, and herself as managing director, she formed the South London Dwellings Company and threw herself into the task of creating "Model Dwellings for Working Folk."

It did not take Miss Cons long to discover that the most immediate cause of misery and squalor in her district was intemperance, nor that the principal focus of intemperance was a rough, tough music hall, the Royal Victoria, known locally as The Old Vic. She went there and found the entertainment rowdy and vulgar. But the entertainment was no more than a cover-up for the more profitable and sinister trade of the saloon. The theatre was living upon "wet money" and its saloon was not just a drinking place, it was also the chief place of assignation in the neighborhood. It was here that prostitutes could be picked up.

We are accustomed to think of the English mid-Victorian spinster as a mousy little person who pressed wildflowers, embroidered smoking-caps for dear Papa and was much given to fits of the vapors. Miss Cons was a very mousy little person indeed and was dreadfully shocked by the goings-on at the Old Vic. But did she run away from the horrid, wicked Old Vic? Did she throw up her little mittened hands and take the vapors? She did not. She took action. She bought the dump, lock, stock and barrel—more particularly barrel.

Following the pattern of her housing project, she formed a wealthy and distinguished committee, which dressed the window and provided the money. Miss Cons was the inconspicuous Hon. Sec. and did the work. In 1880 the Old Vic closed and then, a few months later, reopened with the formidable title of Royal Victoria Coffee Music Hall with a policy that stated "a purified entertainment shall be given and no intoxicants sold." It need hardly be added that this enterprise got almost immediately into financial difficulties.

At the end of eight months, the committee, faced with an alarming balance-sheet, was for throwing in the sponge. Miss Cons argued that the work was only a financial, not a moral, failure—no mention was made of artistic success or failure— that the committee was responsible for a charitable not a business project, and that its clear duty was to put its hand into its pocket and keep right on losing money. Her energy and passion carried the day; her evangelical noblemen pouted but coughed up.

The financial difficulties naturally persisted. The purified entertainment never, as they say, got off the ground. Every committee meeting was a battle and poor Miss Cons must often have wished that she were back in the stained glass studios, or even in the comparative calm of the South London Dwellings Company. Why, oh why, had she ventured up to her neck in the perilous waters of theatrical management?

But now let us leave the aunt and return to the niece.

The younger sister of Emma Cons, Miss Liebe Cons, was a soprano of meager attainment. She married a baritone named Newton Baylis, and he sang none too well either. Their union was financially unsatisfactory but, at the same time, a biological triumph. It was almost alarmingly fertile. It was not only the economics of the Old Vic which caused anxiety to Aunt Emma.

Eventually it was decided that Mr. and Mrs. Newton Baylis and their troop of youngsters might do better in Africa. Relatives clubbed together to provide the fare: London to Cape Town—one way. The early eighteen nineties saw them wandering about the Veldt in a bullock-cart, offering their vaudeville act, The Musical Baylises, to all comers. They fetched up in Johannesburg, where the act seems to have folded. The Musical Baylises quit the boards forever and the financial mainstay of the family became the eldest daughter, Lilian, now in her late teens. She earned an excellent living teaching dancing and the mandolin.

Lilian, however, was overworking. She became gravely ill and Aunt Emmie in London wired to Johannesburg, offering Lilian her return fare if the sea voyage, rest and change and a glimpse of home would do her good. While at home she could undertake light secretarial duties for her aunt in return for her keep.

What follows can best be told in Lilian's own words: "I came home and found my aunt very overworked and ill; and, when I was convalescent, Aunt Ellen, Miss Martineau and Miss Everest [sister and intimate friends of Miss Cons] all urged me to take over management of the Vic, as the much-sought-for right person had never yet materialized. They felt that my experience in organizing concerts in England and South Africa would be a valuable asset to the Vic; and after much consideration I consented. I had intended to return to my parents and take up again my very profitable teaching on the Rand; but when I saw how things stood, I felt it my duty to stay and be of help to Emmie. From that time forward I made my home with my aunts [Emma and Ellen Cons]; I started work as manager of the Vic at a salary of £1 a week."

If ever a round peg stepped into a round hole, it was Lilian Baylis when she accepted Aunt Emma's offer of that job.

Things at the Royal Victoria Coffee Music Hall began to hum. Young Miss Baylis hotted up the coffee and took a shot at hotting up the purified entertainment. Here she reckoned without her Governors. The evangelical peers, the do-good ladies, the representatives of charitable trusts, who formed the governing body had been staunch adherents. Time and again they had plunged their hands into their purses and bailed the

Coffee Music Hall out of Queer Street. But they were doing this because they conceived it their duty to uplift the struggling masses, and, more particularly, to scotch the Demon Rum. And now, here was a young person from the colonies, with alarming energy, a common accent and a domineering manner, who was insisting that the programs at the Coffee Music Hall were dull; that clergymen giving lantern-lectures about the Holy Land were dull; that the Weekly Temperance Rally was *dull*; that dear old Sir Fudley Dudley's lecture on Electro-Magnetism, with a machine which gave deserving lads a tiny shock, was DULL; that the Sunday Concert, with semi-ladies and semi-gentlemen gathered in semi-evening dress around a semi-grand piano singing semi-sacred melodies was DULL.

It does not seem to have occurred to anybody that the Coffee Music Hall lacked an artistic policy, that purity and temperance are not perhaps best served by a program whose sole merit is the negative one of avoiding impurity and discouraging intemperance. Miss Cons, trained as an artist and evidently a person of great intelligence, does not seem to have been at all interested in the artistic quality of the programs. Her attention was entirely focused upon the social and moral aspects of her work.

Lilian Baylis was not nearly such a well-educated or cultivated woman as her aunt. Her schooling had been scrappy and brief. Although, as a member of The Musical Baylises, she had some practical training in music and some experience as a performer, no one could say that she was either a very gifted or at all a cultured musician. But, call it revelation or intuition or just plain good sense, she saw, as Miss Cons and her Governors had never seen, that, if the Old Vic were to be useful, a positive artistic approach was no less important than positive convictions about moral and social reform. Therefore, when Miss Baylis endeavored to fan into flames the moribund embers of the Coffee Music Hall she was met by the unanimous and horrified resistance of her Board.

She was not, however, the type to be daunted by a little

opposition. She had faced tougher difficulties and rougher opponents at her dancing-classes on the Rand, where her pupils had mostly been gold miners. Besides, she had an important ally—Almighty God.

It was hard for those who did not share her simple and fundamental belief to understand it. It was hard not to be exasperated, and at times rather cynically amused, at the way in which she seemed to have God in her pocket. But no one with any sensibility could fail to be moved with reverence and respect for her faith; and no one with any sense would underestimate its formidable power. Miss Baylis had been told by God that the Old Vic audience must have the best. My People—the audience immediately became My People, an assumption half-motherly, half-royal—must have the best. If they were not fobbed off with trash, My People would unerringly recognize the best, be it in music, drama, literature, science or anything else; they needs must love the highest when they saw it, not perhaps at first, but eventually. It was part of her remarkable character that she never seriously troubled about discovering what was the best, or why it was so. She believed that it would be declared to her by Divine Revelation. Such revelations might occur in dreams, in a leading article in the *South London Gazette,* through the mouth of some good man or woman, like the curate at Saint Anne's, or the person who kept the flowerstall on the corner of Linden Avenue and Tibbett's Road. Such revelations might suddenly occur during the course of conversation with a member of her staff, with the policeman on point duty or with a perfect stranger in a railway carriage. I don't think it ever occurred to her that the best, as revealed by her God to Lilian Baylis, could possibly differ from any other revelation by any other God to anyone else; if so, *her* revelation would certainly be the true one. It was the key to her greatness.

God told Miss Baylis that, if the Old Vic program were to be partly musical then the music must be the best. He then, rather surprisingly, added that the best in music is grand opera

—hardly the orthodox view, but there it was. So My People had to have grand opera.

Quite undaunted by the staggering expense and difficulty involved, she proposed to her Governors the formation of a grand opera company. The proposal struck them as not merely impractical but exceedingly sinful. It took her literally years of unremitting, boring, discouraging labor to drive the thin ends of wedges through their prejudice. Then years more were spent in raising her opera company from its tiny, amateur and wholly unsubsidized beginnings until after two decades she had built up not only an extremely respectable professional ensemble—principals, chorus and orchestra—but also an immensely appreciative and sufficiently discriminating audience.

Meantime, a few years after the formation of her opera company and long before it had attained either standard or celebrity, the thought occurred to Miss Baylis that, while she certainly was trying hard to give My People the best in music, the same was not being done in drama.

She took the problem to God. The answer came back pretty quick that Shakespeare was the best in drama. This time the Governors raised no objection. Shakespeare, though an expensive nuisance to produce, is unassailably respectable; besides they had probably realized by now that once God had told Miss Baylis what to do, there really was no point in opposing their joint will.

The Old Vic Shakespeare company was launched in the summer of 1914 with the clouds of war already darkening the sky. It survived the war, began to attract the best serious actors in the profession, and, jointly with the opera, the best audience in the world—young, eager, intelligent, intensely aware and proud of its responsibility as an audience, intensely identified with its favorite players, singers and the theatre of its choice.

It must be remembered, however, that though business for both the operatic and the Shakespearean productions was very large, the prices were very low. The Old Vic was legally constituted as a charity under a charter from Her Majesty's Charity

Commissioners. The charter (1880) governs both the artistic policy: "The theatre shall be used for performance . . . suited for the recreation and instruction of the poorer classes" and the economy as well: "Admission shall not be gratuitous, but shall be at such prices as will make the performances available for artisans and laborers." In the 1920's this was interpreted by the Governors as permitting them to charge five shillings for the best seats (somewhat less than half the equivalent at the time in the West End of London) and sixpence for the gallery.

At such prices, and having to maintain the resources necessary for even the most stringently economical productions of opera and Shakespeare, the business could never be profitable. Even if the house was, and it nearly always was, very full, annual expenditure always exceeded annual income, and usually exceeded also the various charitable gifts and allowances which were made. Miss Baylis was forced to maintain an unceasing vigilance upon her staff, growling like a bulldog at the expenditure of every halfpenny, while, at the same time, like the curate of a poor parish, she had to make humiliating supplication for the bounty of those who could afford it. Meanwhile with jumble sales and the like she screwed a few extra pence out of the pockets of the faithful.

By the end of the nineteen twenties a new problem arose out of the very success of the opera and drama companies. They had expanded beyond the limits of a single building. At this period they shared the bill at the Old Vic. Opera played about five performances each week, drama about three. It was felt that each now commanded an audience large enough to play eight performances weekly; not to do so was, therefore, wildly uneconomic. Moreover each company was now considerably larger than the theatre could conveniently hold. The overcrowding in the dressing rooms and confusion backstage were calamitous. Expansion was essential, but there was no capital to finance it. Miss Baylis took this dilemma to God, and God took it by the horns and commanded her to buy another theatre. He did not, however, reveal a source of capital, so the new theatre had to be bought very cheap.

Sadler's Wells was derelict. It was a barn of a theatre in the rather dreary part of London which lies to the Southeast of King's Cross Station and Holloway Jail. Miss Baylis bought it for a song but was faced with a large expenditure in putting it into workable condition. This was in 1928. Thirty years later the organization had still not completely paid off the debts then incurred. Sadler's Wells, however, made it physically possible for the opera and Shakespeare companies to expand. Shakespeare was played at the Old Vic, with its somewhat smaller stage and capacity. The opera went to the Wells. And soon after, the tiny group of dancers which performed in those operas demanding ballet, was expanded by the brilliant and far-seeing young ballet directress, Ninette de Valois. Gradually a repertoire of ballet was prepared. Fifteen years later, at the end of the Second World War, Miss de Valois removed her Ballet from Sadler's Wells to become, as The Royal Ballet, part of the newly-formed Covent Garden ensemble. With greatly increased financial resources she has been able to make it a justly world-renowned institution and to offer to British dancers a more interesting and less insecure professional career than dancers have enjoyed anywhere in the world, except in Russia.

In 1963, after many years of indecision and laissez-faire, the British Government decided to endow a National Theatre. This was done by incorporating the Old Vic, whose governors parted with their now considerable assets and public goodwill to further the new and more ambitious scheme. Currently, pending the building of its own theatre, which cannot be completed for several years, the National Theatre Company is housed at the Old Vic.

Meantime Sadler's Wells continues as the home of an opera company operating in the vernacular and on a more intimate scale than Covent Garden but with no lower an artistic standard. It is now recognized as part of the National Opera complex

and receives considerable annual subsidy from both the Arts
Council of Great Britain and the London County Council.

Thus, thirty years after her death, stands the work of Lilian
Baylis.

Ninette de Valois

Ninette de Valois was the name chosen by a romantic Irish
mother for a teen-aged girl who was beginning as a professional
dancer. A more unsuitable label could hardly have been attached to this practical, decisive, realistic and gloriously honest
person. Her real name, which was Edris Stannus, and is now
Edris Connell, is perfect.

At a very early age she was principal dancer in the Lyceum
Pantomime in London. Various engagements of similar character followed, in pantomime and musical comedy, in London
and on the road. She was far too good for the work she was
doing. But already, though she was unaware of it, this dreary
professional experience was shaping her for the career which lay
ahead.

There followed a period with the Diaghilev Ballet. It was
brief but highly influential. It gave new impetus to artistic
enthusiasm which was beginning to wilt; it set for her new standards; the very weaknesses in the Diaghilev organization stimulated her very active and very Irish critical and rebellious
faculties.

After this followed a few years when she did part-time
choreographic work for the Abbey Theatre in Dublin, notably
on Yeats' plays for dancers; and similar part-time work at the
Festival Theatre in Cambridge. She also taught and formed
a small group of dancers under her own direction.

I first met her at Cambridge, when for a few seasons I directed the Festival Theatre. Miss de Valois and her group
gave occasional Dance Matinees—ten or twelve short pieces
in front of black velvet curtains. One was struck by her own

wonderfully, almost excessively, clear-cut technique and the disciplined, intelligent marshalling of rather scanty resources.

A year or two later she was working for Miss Baylis at the Old Vic, putting on dances where they were required in the Shakespearean or operatic productions. At this time the opera worked with a voluntary corps de ballet—office girls who came in at the end of their day's work and were rewarded with a sausage roll and a glass of lemonade. In 1930 Miss Baylis opened Sadler's Wells, a large theatre in North London, as a sort of counterpart to the Old Vic in South London. The opera was established at Sadler's Wells, the larger of the two theatres, and Miss Baylis was persuaded by Miss de Valois to allow the formation, on a shoestring budget, of a small ballet company.

This was the beginning of what was first of all known as the Vic-Wells Ballet. When enquiries became persistent about the identity of a mythical Mr. Vic Wells, the name was changed to Sadler's Wells Ballet. Finally, when its activities were transferred to Covent Garden, and with the granting of a royal charter, it became known as The Royal Ballet.

From the beginning the ballet has borne and, though she has now retired from active control, will long continue to bear, the personal impress of Ninette de Valois—"Madame," as she is now affectionately and respectfully known to hundreds of past and present members of her company. It is the impress not so much of a great artist as a great general. All the moves by which the company was inexorably transported from its lowly and impoverished beginnings to world fame and world standard, all these moves were planned like a chess-game and executed with scrupulous fairness, honesty and the absence of vulgar self-seeking, which disfigures so much theatrical endeavor. It has been far more than the creation of a repertoire and of a company of dancers. She has created conditions in which the career of the British dancer has been completely revolutionized. The elaborate, exhausting technical training is not allowed to stunt intellectual and social life. I guess from her own early experience she has learned how stultifying it can be to dance in worthless entertainments, which nevertheless call for every ounce of energy and prodigious skill as well.

The most significant part of the Royal Ballet Organization, if not that best known to the public, is the system of training in its school, with graduated entry into a company, which over the years has developed not only artistic traditions, but, equally important, traditions of service to the community and loyalty of its members to the organization.

There are others who admire the art of Ninette de Valois, as opposed to her generalship, more fervently than I. *Job* I consider her masterpiece. It attempts to say something serious and interesting, possibly a little beyond what I may be wrong in regarding as the narrow limits of the dancer's art. *Rake's Progress* and *Checkmate* have been much admired, but I find them rather too obviously and symmetrically organized, efficient rather than interesting.

She has considered it important to relate her modern repertoire to, and to base her company's technique upon, the so-called classics of ballet—the works of Petipa to scores of Tchaikovsky, Fokine's *Les Sylphides* and some of the important works of the Diaghilev repertoire. In principle this is fine. In practice I think it has resulted in a re-creation of the mechanics, the technique, the outward manifestation of these works, while too often their spirit and meaning has been missed. This, I think, is the reverse of de Valois' great qualities. Her decisive efficiency sees the need of a classical basis. But to see *why* a work is a classic and to reproduce the spirit and feeling which make it so, that is work for an artist, not a general. It would be too much to expect of any great general, even a great lady-general, that artistic and feeling qualities should exactly balance the generalship.

The monument stands. Her Royal Ballet will, under successive directors, change its character, sometimes for the better, sometimes for the worse. That is inevitable in the case of an institution. It is de Valois' achievement to have created out of the fragments, the odds and undignified ends of a neglected and undervalued craft, an institution which reflects her own disciplined energy, high intelligence and sense of serious purpose.

Laurence Olivier

Laurence Olivier is the son of a clergyman. In his youth he was a choirboy and went to a choir school. This means that two dominant influences on his formative years were music and liturgy. His theatrical career began when he was still very young at the Birmingham Repertory Theatre. His talent was immediately apparent. Before he was thirty he had played leading parts in London and New York; in a famous production of *Romeo and Juliet* he and John Gielgud alternated in the parts of Romeo and Mercutio.

This was the first time I saw him act. He had been severely faulted by the drama critics for what they regarded as bad verse-speaking. I thought he spoke the verse with marvelous clarity, energy and variety. What more can you want? He had, it is true, a tendency to rant; to make rather exaggerated contrasts of pace, pitch and volume. But these were the excesses of ardent, youthful temperament. Time would cure them. And, anyway, how rare it is to hear someone who really can blow up a storm, whose voice explodes like a bomb, crashes like breaking glass, screams like a macaw. A lot of the noises he made, and still makes, were not "beautiful"; and drama critics, then as now, like their Shakespeare to be sonorous. In the interests of sonority they seem prepared to sacrifice most other values. I will confess that to me the Voice Beautiful is all too often the Voice Dull.

Laurence Olivier is never dull. The voice, however, has more the quality of brass than of strings. And even now, after many years of intense cultivation and ceaseless practice, it is the vigor and brilliance of his tone which impresses. Sweetness does not come so easily. I have never been able to understand those critics who are not aware of the intense musicality which infuses all his performances—a rare sensitivity to rhythm, color, phrasing, pace and pitch.

He has never been a particularly handsome man, but he has always been able, on the stage, to suggest extreme good looks. Partly this is due to skill in make-up, far more to the vitality and intelligence which inform every glance, and the athletic energy and grace of every movement.

He could have had—indeed briefly had—a dazzling career as a movie star. But he has preferred to use the extraordinary opportunities which his gifts have presented, to extend his expressive range rather than his fortune or fan mail. Among his impressive achievements have been his screen versions of Shakespeare's *Henry V, Hamlet* and *Richard III*. In my opinion, none of these was artistically successful. *Henry V* had some splendid moments of action but they had almost no relevance to Shakespeare's text and only helped to emphasize the chasm which separates stage play from screenplay. The achievement was to get these productions onto the screens of the world in the teeth of the timid and mercenary moguls of the film industry. But even Olivier's reputation, skill and formidable determination has not been able to realize his projected screen version of *Macbeth*. Eventually, perhaps, he will make it. But I hope that he will not allow his gifts to be squandered on what must in the nature of things only be a popularization, a reduction, of a masterpiece.

One of the dangers of our times is that with enormously widespread and virtually instantaneous communication of ideas, success becomes overwhelming. There is no longer any possibility for an actor, an author or a musician to be modestly and reasonably successful. He is either practically unknown or else he is a household word from the North Pole to the South, from China to Peru. Successful artists cannot but be distracted by their success. They are too rich, confronted with too many attractive but confusing choices. If you are the object of a great deal of public attention it is difficult not to become self-important and not (even worse) to become nervous, over-anxious to please, afraid to offend.

In thirty years of celebrity Olivier has learned to handle the tricky business graciously and cleverly. But energy has had to be spent on this. I admire his art so wholeheartedly, love him so warmly as a friend and colleague that I grudge this drain upon energy and concentration. I even grudge the time and energy which have to be spent on administrative work for the British National Theatre. Rightfully he is at its head. He was the right figurehead for its inception. He is doing a fine job. But it is not the job he does best. Much of what he is at present doing could be done equally well by several other people, none of whom could play Othello, Macbeth, Lear, Faustus, and a dozen other great parts which, at present, he has not time to think about.

The years are passing. I suppose it is idle to wish it, but I'd like him to be less celebrated, less distinguished, less important and more free.

I want to see him abdicate. I want to see a sign which advertises "Throne Vacant—Will suit hard-working, honest, methodical Monarch."

10. THEATRE IN NEW YORK AS COMPARED TO LONDON

I AM OFTEN ASKED how I think the theatre in New York compares with that in London. Most people think that New York does musicals better than London, and this, in my opinion, is certainly true of American musicals. The London productions of *Oklahoma!*, *Carousel*, *Call Me Madam* or *Guys and Dolls* were but pale poor ghosts of their more robust New York originals. On the other hand, when, occasionally, a British musical is done in New York—*The Boy Friend* for example— it is apt to be a loud, rich travesty of a more subtle and delicate original.

At the present time New York seems to be better served with new plays of some serious interest than is London. Partly no doubt this is because New York, virtually the only producing center of an entire continent, can command a larger aggregate of potential authors. But partly also it is because a play of originality, expressing unconventional ideas or using an unfamiliar technique, stands a far better chance of being produced in New York than in London.

This is not because the New York public is less conventional. That is not at all my impression. It is rather because there are in London three or four dominant managements who control a high proportion of the theatres, and themselves produce a high proportion of the plays. A play which is not acceptable to this very limited number of producers has very little chance of being seen. It is only fair to say that, though this is a bad situation, most of the individuals concerned are both expert and honest. But they are also very conservative. The West End Theatre is operated like a very respectable old-fashioned grocery store.

In New York, on the other hand, anyone can go into management who can scare up a bit of dough. And anyone does. There is plenty of money knocking about; the theatre offers an attractive field for gambling; so that in New York there are plenty of would-be producers with heaps of cash but no theatrical experience, no particular skill or aptitude, nothing but what can politely be described as a flair for the theatre. This situation seems to me to be simultaneously the New York theatre's greatest asset and greatest liability.

On the credit side the flair of amateurs often leads them to back a highly individual fancy; to back those unlikely starters which surprise everyone not merely by winning the race but by being horses of the first quality. On the debit side their lack of experience, and often of administrative competence, makes a shaky scaffolding for any enterprise. More important, the mere fact that there are so many would-be producers engenders a state of intense and anarchic competition—competition for a "success" which is only definable in the misleading and limited terms of numbers of tickets sold.

Under such conditions it is virtually impossible for any producer to think in terms of policy. The proof of the pudding is in the eating. In any New York season many scores of people sponsor theatrical enterprises. Which one of these over the last ten, or even five, or even two seasons, has expressed in a series of productions any policy which could be intelligibly or creditably defined in a single sentence?

Anyone who has had any professional experience on Broadway will testify to the fever of competition. And if confirmation were needed as to anarchy, one has only to examine the contesting claims of the different trade unions involved, each one scrambling for its own members' advantage judged in exclusively selfish terms, with a cynical disregard for any purpose which the theatre may have, or for any service which it might possibly render to the community.

In such a theatre none of the many producers appears able to think in longer terms than his own next opening night. Many of them are highly intelligent and respectable people, aware and resentful of such conditions. But as yet they have evolved no way of escape. I have heard plenty of intelligent damning of the present anarchy, plenty of lip-service to such European institutions as the Comédie Française, the German state theatres, the Old Vic, plenty of sighing for such an institution in New York. Yet, we have recently witnessed the foundering of a repertory project, which, had things turned out differently—and there is, of course, hope that they still might—could well have been the most important theatrical effort of our epoch. There was money, perhaps even too much money; the most eminent managerial and directorial talents were available; a distinguished and influential board governed the policy.

The ship put to sea and encountered stormy weather. Instead of all hands pulling together to defy the storm and grapple with the hundred emergencies which beset a laboring ship, dissension broke out. In all the hubbub it is pointless for outsiders to wonder who was to blame. Better to concentrate on wishing calm seas and prosperous voyage to future captains and new crews.

Why? Mistakes were made. But in all human affairs mistakes are made, and then retrieved and then lived down. I think there can only be one explanation for why this enterprise—as originally conceived—came to grief: those at its head cannot have felt about it passionately. There was not sufficient dedication.

In a buoyant economy, like that of the U.S.A. at present, multitudes, confusing multitudes of attractive opportunities are endlessly presenting themselves to energetic and gifted people. Consequently it is hard to know which to select. The complicated choices use up far too much of the precious energy and talents which should be creatively occupied. Sustained dedication, in my opinion, is not voluntary, but forced by economic circumstances. Lots of us can, and do, dedicate ourselves to a single task, to something which can be accomplished on a single quick enthusiastic impulse, and by a quick violent effort. It is the sustained uphill pull, the keeping of enthusiasm alive over long periods, perhaps years, of fruitlessness and discouragement—it is persistent dedication which is so hard to achieve. With the exception of the great saints, we humans are too weak for the physical, intellectual and moral effort which sustained dedication involves.

I think of the foundation of the only theatrical institution which I know well, the Old Vic in London. Its creation in 1914 was almost entirely due to the dedicated energy of one woman, Lilian Baylis (1874–1937). Her achievement was great, but the effort far greater. She sustained it in the face of a minimum of public encouragement, with the meagerest material reward for more than twenty years. But I hope it is no belittlement of this extraordinary effort to believe that Lilian Baylis was only able to sustain it because her gifts and aspirations had no alternative means of expression; her will was not puzzled by the power of choice.

I feel that in present circumstances in New York all the potential founders of an American counterpart to the Comédie Française or the Old Vic are confused by this power of choice. While so many alternative offers are available, none of the leading practitioners can be reasonably expected to dedicate himself to a single, extremely heavy, probably ungrateful and certainly prolonged task.

In present circumstances such dedication will only be assumed by a Great Saint. And I cannot believe that to put a Great Saint in command of a theatre, or for that matter a ship, or any other kind of community, is an idea likely to commend itself except in case of dire emergency, when society needs his exceptional strength, his vision, his singleness of purpose. In circumstances of ease and comfort, such as America is at present enjoying, the Great Saint would be an intolerable bore and a continuous reproach to our own weakness and venality.

I look for no remission of the present state of anarchy, until there is less general contentment with the status quo, until, in fact, things aren't so rich and comfortable and easy for so many of us. Then, and then only, will there be the necessary reconsideration of values and purposes. Then, and then only, will there be a possibility of some individual, or small group of individuals, finding their energies and aspirations forced by economic circumstances into the single and restricted channel which alone can generate a current of sufficient force.

Have I given the impression that, in contrast to anarchy in New York, the British theatre is perfectly governed? I hope not. The British theatre has, however, in the Old Vic, now the National Theatre, an important bulwark against capitalist cartels and competitive anarchy. It is noteworthy that the state support dates from 1941. It was only in the most difficult and dangerous period of the war, when the bombs were raining upon London, when, incidentally, the Old Vic itself had been heavily damaged by enemy action, when Britain was fighting virtually alone—it was only in this emergency that Britannia decided that an institutionalized theatre presenting the classics was a *necessity* which no civilized community could afford to be without.

11. IS THERE MADNESS
IN "THE METHOD"?

THE METHOD has for some time been the most talked-about approach to acting in the American theatre; its temple is the Actors' Studio, its high priest is Lee Strasberg. The Actors' Studio has attracted some distinguished adherents; some extravagant claims for it are advanced with ardor and as warmly rebutted. It has been a valuable force for thought and discussion about the art of the theatre, about the craft of acting and about the philosophy and technique of self-expression. Its influence is widely felt in contemporary acting, not just in New York, but in every English-speaking theatre. That cannot be questioned. The value and the permanence of this influence are a matter of controversy.

Let me begin by saying that I have no first-hand experience of the Method. I have met and worked with zealous Methodists; I have heard descriptions of rehearsals and demonstrations of the Method; but I have never attended any of the gospel meetings.

I am under the impression that Lee Strasberg, a wonderful teacher, is inculcating an approach to acting derived from that of Stanislavsky, the founder and director of the Moscow Art Theatre. The basis of this is that the actor must base his characterization upon his own personal experience. He must imagine a given situation so strongly that he can "feel" himself in it. His own experience being necessarily limited, he must also feel it legitimate to derive at second-hand from the real experience of other people, but not from other acting.

With little of this could any sensible person disagree. My own disagreement with the Method is limited, and under two heads: theoretically, it is in rebellion against conditions which have ceased to exist and, consequently, is out of date. Practically, it places too much emphasis upon self-analysis and too little upon technique.

Let us first consider the theoretical side.

The theatrical context, in reaction to which Stanislavsky founded the Moscow Art Theatre and his own acting method, belonged to the *fin de siècle* and the very early years of the twentieth century, and no longer exists. It has been liquidated by the social, political and economic revolutions which have occurred all over the world. Stanislavsky was reacting against a theatre which was still concerned to please an audience of the socially élite and its imitators—a theatre very concerned with inherited conventions, derived from the Parisian boulevard comedies and dramas which had dominated Europe for more than a century. Stanislavsky preached a method based upon first-hand observation, rather than upon imitation of other acting. He also advocated the production of plays which reflected contemporary Russian life in a real way, rather than as a romantic image of elegant manners abroad. The Moscow Art Theatre, while not at all political, was nevertheless strongly nationalist.

Although it was not at first of any great popular or commercial account—the theatre was tiny and by no means always full—the Moscow Art Theatre became the most powerful influence on the stage of its time. The "poetic naturalism" of Chekhov, in supplement to the prosaic and didactic quality of Ibsen and Shaw, has been the dominant influence on serious playwrights of the last fifty years, not only in Russia but all over the occidental world; the acting and direction at the Moscow Art are still the dominant models, although possibly a little less so now, since the impact of Bertolt Brecht.

Stanislavsky did not really hit the American theatre until after the publication in English of his book *My Life in Art*. He then found enthusiastic disciples in Mr. Strasberg and Harold

Clurman, founders, in 1931, of the Group Theatre. The Group, like the Moscow Art before it, found itself in reaction against the theatrical status quo. It was opposed to the conventional themes and methods of the commercial theatre, which to the young people of the Group seemed extremely reactionary. It was opposed also to foreign domination of the American stage, particularly by London's West End, with its insistence upon elegance and gentility to the exclusion of almost all other content.

This was the period of depression, the end of one epoch and the beginning of many radically new political, social and economic ideas. The Group Theatre was in the avant-garde of this ferment, and I hope that a non-American may be forgiven for emphasizing something which in subsequent political ferments has been either overlooked or misinterpreted: this literary and theatrical movement was an earnest and conscious expression of American nationalism. The Group was trying, early in the comparatively brief history of the American theatre, to look at indigenous American problems and characters through American eyes, and to express them in an indigenous way, not in a manner imitative of dominant—and imported—conventions.

Harold Clurman, in *The Fervent Years,* one of the best books of theatrical reminiscences which I know, has described the aims, impact and some of the inner stresses and strains of the Group. Its activity, compared to that of the Moscow Art Theatre, was confined to a very brief period. Its artistic achievement has been less than its influence. The Group, I venture to believe, has been an all-important influence in the evolution of the Method. The ideas which brought the Group into being are the source of the Method's greatest value; but I suggest that they still express youthful revolt against a social and political environment which has now ceased to exist.

In 1931 there was some point in young actors and actresses proclaiming by their dress, speech and bearing that they were of the proletariat. In 1931, there was some important political and social purpose to be served by depicting faithfully the efforts of the inarticulate American masses to express themselves. In 1931, this required some serious political faith, not in Leninism, but in the future of American democracy. Artistically it was ground which, outside Russia, had hardly been trodden, and demanded a serious effort to evolve a new technique, because the current fashions in acting and directing were no guide.

Today the burning issues of the 1930's are ashes, and other issues are on fire. Even in America, comparatively so little affected by the events of 1939–45 (a fact which is to many Americans bewilderingly hard to grasp, so accustomed are they to believe themselves in the vanguard rather than the rear guard of historical context), the political, social and economic changes have been immense. Meantime, the young iconoclasts of the early Odets period are now middle-aged; the prominent ones are well-to-do and securely seated upon the very thrones under which a generation ago they were placing the dynamite. But the Method-ists do not seem to have quite got around to this.

In blue jeans, with dirty nails and wild hair, the Methodists are busy proclaiming themselves proletarian—but members of a vintage Proletariat. While in 1931 it was new, and even dangerous, for artists to announce that they were also proletarians, it is now cliché—especially when more than one prominent associate of the Method has been at pains to dissociate this type of artistic proletarianism from any taint of political subversion, from the faintest tinge of red. In 1931, to adequately present an inarticulate proletarian upon the stage required some innovation of acting technique; but this too has now become cliché.

This brings me to the second issue on which I part company with the Method: technique. In 1931, it was necessary to seek new means of expressing new ideas about people whom it was a novelty to see depicted on the stage. Until then, stage conventions had required that, with amazingly few exceptions, plays were about the Upper Orders. If members of the Lower Orders appeared at all, it was as character parts—Faithful Retainers, Roughs, Prostitutes, Little Matchgirls or, most frequently, just Comics. Then plays began to have as their chief figures Taxi Drivers and Boxers shown, not as the expression of natures more rough and inarticulate than their former betters, but as people who had been denied the privileges of the more fortunate.

It can readily be seen that the new school of playwriting required a new school of acting, less conventional, less romantic, less elegant, but, in compensation, more real. Now, oddly enough, most of us in the theatre, as in other avocations, are nearer in environment to the proletariat than to Grand Dukes. Hence, when the new school required of the actor that he unlearn a lot of fancy ways and fancy speech, which had been thought necessary in the portrayal of Grand Dukes, it seemed as if he were being required to revert to behaviorism, to just being himself.

Incidentally, isn't it just middle-class sentimentality, and a very superior attitude, to imagine that it is more real to be rough than to be genteel, more real to wear blue jeans than a neat Ivy League number, more real to look like a whore than a Junior Miss? Surely it is not more real, but less expensive. The proletariat does not dress and speak and behave as it does, nor live where it does, from choice, but because it cannot afford to do otherwise. In America today it is only eccentric intellectuals who are "prole" by choice.

In 1931, however, the Group believed that good acting consisted in being yourself and, consistently enough, aimed to make its members better actors by making them more aware of themselves. Remember that this epoch coincided with the first great popular impact of psychoanalysis. At the confluence of two rivers—popular psychology and behaviorist acting—like Pittsburgh, stood the Group. At the same confluence stands the Method. But roughly three decades have passed and the waters of both streams are now less turbulent, but also far less clear and fresh.

In my opinion, the Method now means behaviorist acting, which is cliché and which is inadequate to express any wide range, either of character, environment or style. It is suited only to express the very limited field of the actor's own, and his friends' experience, and in a naturalistic style. It is stylish acting (by which I do not, of course, mean merely elegant) which now needs cultivation.

The search by actors for the truth within themselves has now gone too far. They are in grave danger of forgetting two more objective elements of truth, which no artist should dare to ignore: First, each of us is not only himself, but a member of the human race; second, it is the duty of an artist to develop the means of communication of the truth within himself, so as to share it with fellow members of the race. The Methodists overprize the search for truth as opposed to the revelation of truth. They have neglected the means of communication.

Now the actor's principal means of expression is the voice. The expression of eyes, of the whole body, is important, too, but it is on the breathstream and by means of sounds and, more particularly, the organization of sounds into, first, syllables, then words, then sentences, that the most subtle and the most articulate communication occurs between human creatures.

Until recently the Actors' Studio has tended to pay but little attention to matters of technique. But now Mr. Strasberg has said that this has been a mistake. Lessons in voice production and diction are now part of the curriculum. It is a radically new idea that anything so self-conscious and artificial as vocal technique, so unspontaneous, so remote from the animal life of the individual, or the social life of the group, should be admissible as part of the Method. And so influential has the Method become in the contemporary theatre that it is going to be very hard to eradicate the notion that any cultivation of this craft can only be to the detriment, not only of an actor's art, but of his psyche.

This notion has led the Methodists into one very awkward dilemma: none of the great classics of the theatre—the Greek tragedies, French tragedy, Shakespeare, Molière, Schiller or Goethe, Ibsen or Shaw—can be adequately performed without a real battery of technical accomplishment. An untrained beginner, however gifted, just cannot do justice to great rhetorical poetry any more than an untrained beginner in music can sit right down and play a Bach fugue.

So far the Method has not suggested that it aims beyond a very highly developed behaviorism. I am not denying that in this field remarkable results have been achieved. But mere behaviorism will not take an actor far on the way to King Lear, Andromache or Faust.

I guess that a great deal is talked and written about the Method by persons, including myself, who have only been indirectly concerned with it. And while this is not quite fair, it is absolutely inevitable. The Method is a popular talking-point, and, as such, has gained extraordinary prestige. But fame and success carry their own penalties as well as rewards. That Marlon Brando and others have been associated with them has been, in one sense, a great boost for the Actors' Studio; but in another it has been detrimental. Not all its gifted alumni can be described as accomplished actors; their fame rests upon other qualities. And the sort of publicity which their connection has generated has blown up a serious professional effort into a sensational stunt, with many of the stigmata of quackery.

To sum up: it is my opinion that Mr. Strasberg is a serious teacher. The Actors' Studio is genuinely and laudably trying to break away from theatrical clichés, but has gone too far in the direction of self-analysis, and away from a sensible pursuit of craftsmanship, particularly vocal technique. The great professional and popular success of the Method has resulted in a rather grave lack of humility on the part of many of its adherents. Statements on the lines of the classics being all bunk are not unusual, and there's a tendency to forget that people of my age do not find anything new in the theory. On the contrary, we remember when it was new to us in the mouth of

Stanislavsky; people a little older remember the same theories being applied still earlier at the Abbey Theatre in Dublin and in the folk theatres all over Europe; still older people recall Shaw's *Quintessence of Ibsenism*. And so on, back and back.

Looking forward, I see reason to believe that, like every popular craze and like so many progressive movements whose adherents become unduly excited by success, today's Method may all too easily become tomorrow's dodo.

12. DOMINANT DIRECTOR

IT IS OFTEN said that today's theatre is a director's theatre. Hardly less often a supplementary statement follows: that the modern director has got above his station, is too big for his boots.

It is true that the director of a play now draws more attention than used to be the case. I suppose when it became apparent that in the movies the director was the dominant influence —even more important than the actors, far more important than the author, who has never rated higher in movies than a very minor functionary—it was then that public and critics began to wonder whether in the theatre as well this creature might not exert a certain influence.

The director has been prominent at least since Sophocles directed the chorus in the first performance of *Oedipus Rex*. After all, a play requires the assembly and arrangement of many component parts, the coordination of many different skills. Without direction, the process of production would be anarchy.

A rose by any other name would smell as sweet; so maybe a director by any other name—stage-manager, producer, *metteur-en-scène, régisseur*—might stink less. The most romantic and best loved directors have been, I suppose, the great actor-managers.

In the English-speaking theatre the greatest of these, and almost the last, was Sir Henry Irving. His reign at the Lyceum Theatre in London (1878–1902) not only was long but also was marked by consistently high purpose and distinguished achievement. Suppose that an artist of no less integrity and efficiency were living now, could he possibly rival Irving's achievement? I think not. To begin with, the expenses and risks of theatrical management are now incredibly greater—the salaries of actors and staff, the charges for rent and services have risen in higher percentage than the rise in ticket prices. Also, when Irving made a profit, he did not surrender more than the tiniest fraction to the tax collector. Too, he operated in an incredibly simpler framework. To give but a single instance, Irving was not faced with incessant wrangles with six different trade unions.

But now the functions that eighty years ago could be performed almost single-handed by an Irving, are devolved upon a number of different individuals—a manager, or producer, with several aides, a director, publicity men, accountants, insurance agents—a hierarchy in which the actor, though still the most publicized and probably the best loved, is no longer the most powerful figure.

I have often heard senior actors, and especially senior actresses, sigh for the good old days of the actor-manager, and incidentally disparage the bad new days of the dominant director: "Ah, my dear, when I was a gel, I went down to my first rehearsal and as Sir James handed me the script he said: 'This is *your* scene, young lady; where should you like to stand?'"

But I wonder if the young lady will really have fared better in the hands of dear old Sir James than in the less courtly paw of a modern director. If she had any sense at all in her pretty head she would hardly have said to Sir James that she would like to stand plumb in the center of the stage and plumb in the focus of the brightest light, while he, dear, good old man, stood in a dark corner with his back to the audience. Not at all. She would have said, and very properly: "I shall stand wherever you, Sir James, in your wisdom and experience, decree." And she might very well have added that wherever she stood the audience would be looking not at herself, a personable but negligible beginner, but at the great Sir James; and, further, that if she did stand center stage in the light, with Sir James downstage in the dark, the old fox knew six different but infallible ways of drawing the audience's attention off her and onto himself.

A more serious drawback to the dominance of the director is the possibility that he may override the author of the play. Recently there have been two *causes célèbres*—I will name no names—involving the same director in charges of overriding the will of two different authors and staging *his*, not their, versions of their plays.

Naturally, I cannot on this point pretend to impartiality. I stand by the side of my fellow director, and I argue thus: If an author believes that his play is being mishandled he can demand the director's resignation. If this course is contractually impossible, he can still withdraw his own name and authority from this particular production and make a rumpus in which, if he plays his cards with any skill at all, he cannot but cut a sympathetic and dignified figure.

I strongly suspect that in the instances we are considering matters never came near to such a crux. There was some good-tempered argument; the director, as the more experienced technician and the more dominant personality, prevailed. The authors, after the event and without rancor, allowed it to be known that they had been overridden. Gossip blew the whole business up into a scandal in which a Wicked Uncle had gobbled up two darling, talented little Babes in the Wood.

Throughout theatrical history authors have been browbeaten, if not by directors then by leading actors or tycoons or artistic noblemen. Further, it is not just dramatists who are the victims of dominant interference. Consider the literary men who have altered sonnets, epics, novels, works of science, history and philosophy to comply with the demands of wife, mistress, publisher, the bar-keep on the corner, the secretary of the golf club, the twins who will be twelve next October. Why, good gracious, Edward Lear used to make drastic alterations to works of genius in order to please his cat! And—here's the point

—he thought by doing so he made them more geniusy. And very possibly he was right.

Every script is, theoretically, susceptible to improvement. The fact that words, or thoughts have been written down, even printed, does not make them wise or sacred. Even masterpieces can be improved in certain contexts. I plead guilty, without the slightest twinge of conscience, to making cuts in the text of *Hamlet;* even more outrageous, to adding a few lines to the text of *All's Well That Ends Well.* My lines, in undistinguished but unpretentious blank verse, make clear an otherwise obscure moment in the story, have been used in two different productions of the play and, to the best of my knowledge, have never been spotted by anyone, except the small-part actors to whom they were allotted.

Such liberties are not, of course, to be taken lightly. They may from time to time be justified, but they are *liberties.* But, and here again is the point, such liberties are not the exclusive privilege of theatrical directors. They are the privilege of anyone who thinks and cares enough to take them. And they are taken, incidentally, by every reader who skips a line or two of obviously dull matter, every editor who paraphrases what is obscure, every scholar who dares to amend what he believes to be a misprint—"a babbled of green fields" instead of "a table of green fields."

In general, however, I will not deny that in the current theatre the director's prestige has become over-inflated. Half the plays on Broadway, in any given season, could be as well performed without the services of a director—and, were the truth known, half of them are. But that is not to say that someone has not done all the organizational chores that are a part of the craft, although they have little connection with the art, of theatrical direction.

But difficult, important or significant plays do require direction; that is to say the elucidation of the text, the imposition of a musical and choreographic pattern on the acting and, above all, the pulling together into a unity of what would otherwise be a series of isolated, even contradictory, impulses and impressions.

You might think that the best person to direct a play would be its author. So he would be, but for three rather important considerations. First, authors are apt to love their brain-children not wisely but too well, and, like all parents, are not usually the most impartial or best judges of their character and quality. Second, authors rarely combine a good working knowledge of their craft with a good working knowledge of the quite different craft of direction. Third, the authors of most of the plays that really *demand* the author's presence at rehearsal, are unavoidably prevented from being there by a previous engagement which not even the greatest of mortals can decline.

13. TRIBUTE TO AGE

PLAYS WRITTEN by experienced authors rarely demand much of youth. The leading parts are designed to fit actors and actresses at the peak of their powers, whose names are well known to the public—people, that is to say, somewhere between the ages of thirty-five and sixty-five.

Under flattering and powerful lights, under thick layers of grease paint (that interesting and significant survival of the classic mask) it is possible for leading actors to go on year after year, decade after decade, "looking much the same," suggesting an indefinite but attractive age, not young but certainly not old.

These are the players who carry the brunt of the evening, with whom the audience is asked to identify itself. Around them, to eke out the story, will be younger and older persons. In the stage jargon, which has passed from ham to ham across the centuries, these two categories, the young and the old, are known as "juvenile" and "character."

You might suppose that it was all plain sailing and nice and sensible and logical, that beginners would begin as juveniles and then, after an apprenticeship of ten or fifteen years in the tennis-racket-swinging, perfunctory-little-love-scene department, would, if good enough, graduate to leading parts. And then, in the fullness of time, step back into the lesser responsibility and exertion of character roles.

But life is never sensible and logical; and the theatre is a highlighted, overstrung microcosm of life, where all its illogicalities and contradictions, noble as well as absurd, are seen as under a magnifying glass.

Beginners are only cast as juveniles if they are pretty and shapely and strongly suggest that they are nice and normal. Since most of us are plain and decidedly odd, few of us get asked to be juveniles. As a beginner I was positively weird, and made my debut, bearded to the knees, as a sea captain of eighty.

In the folklore of Broadway there is a legend that the American public puts a premium on youth. When I was first concerned with casting a play in New York, the management thought it necessary to rub my nose in this legend.

"Of course, in Europe," they said, "it's touching how loyal the public is to old favorites. Touching."—and the tone allowed me to feel how absurdly, shamefully sentimental such loyalty was—"But here in New York the young parts must be played by young people—fresh, pert, peppy, lively youngsters." And that very evening I was taken to the theatre to see a play called *Romeo and Juliet*.

Here the teen-age heroine was enacted by a fresh, pert, peppy, lively youngster of forty-eight. No one could fail to be impressed with the noble, ample, majestic personality of this lady—a Miss Katharine Cornell, who made no concessions to the niceties of realism, but played the role in her own beautiful, but already gray, hair, and in a stylized, commanding manner that suggested many interesting possibilities but had nothing whatever to do with pertness or pep.

Down the years I have seen in New York, as everywhere else, the same acceptance of quite senior ladies and gentlemen pretending to be anything from ten to thirty years younger than they really were. And this acceptance is not just loyalty. The public wants some guarantee before it lays out money on theatre tickets (a commodity whose price is at present governed by a series of madly, almost criminally inflationary conditions) that the fare is good. The presence of Mr. X or Miss Y in the cast is some guarantee of quality; and who cares if Miss Y likes to play women of thirty-seven, when we all suspect that she is around seventy-three. She plays them so well, and most of the time she really passes for thirty-seven—well, forty-seven.

In opera, ballet and musical comedy youth is more indispensable, because the physical demands in these fields are more considerable than in the so-called straight play. In opera, the voices begin to deteriorate sadly early, especially in the high ranges. Few sopranos remain in the top rank much beyond their early forties. Of course, it is possible to continue in opera much longer in character and buffo roles, where acting is more important than singing. And what an enrichment to an opera company are some of its senior members, who no longer have the least pretentions to "vox"! At the Metropolitan, for instance, Alessio de Paolis, long after he really had any voice at all, brought a lifetime of experience and skill to bear upon the series of amusing, touching and exquisitely wrought miniatures which were his repertoire in his later years.

In ballet the leading dancers are beginning to decline by their mid-thirties. Their career is as short and strenuous as that of a prizefighter. Occasionally a great dancer will remain at the top for much longer—Galina Ulanova, of the Bolshoi Ballet, is well over forty and Margot Fonteyn, of the Royal Ballet, though her art seems utterly untouched by time, has been at the top of the tree lo! these many years.

Isn't it a pity that ballet companies make so little use of older people? I cannot but feel that the works would seem so much more dramatically interesting if the character roles—the aged magicians, the mother empresses, the inhabitants of Fall River, were not all pert and peppy youngsters in fright-wigs.

My own most surprising experience of youth and age in the theatre was with Habimah in Israel, just after the war. For five years the company had been completely cut off from other theatrical influences; for twenty years before that it had existed as an exotic Russian plant in the soil of the Near East. The company was a Zionist offshoot of the Moscow Art Theatre. In Israel its members had been preaching the gospel of Stanislavsky. They had also been growing no younger.

Yet for these people the twenty-five years since they had left

Moscow seemed but the winking of an eye. In make-up, style of acting and production, we seemed to witness miraculously embalmed the very distillation of the intention of Stanislavsky and of his most gifted pupil, Vakhtangov. But over it had fallen the years, which lay like an impalpable gray dust upon the heads of the company.

Old, old ladies and gentlemen were still playing the same leading parts they had played for twenty-five years. Middle-aged heavyweights in gold wigs with the wildest of rose-pink cheeks would spring about in a frenzy of boyish and girlish animation. Meanwhile, the later recruits to the company, and its students, were relegated to the character roles. Eighteen-year-olds, their infant mugs cross-hatched with lines, in busbies of white wool, loaded with canes and ear-trumpets and pince-nezs, would play the grandparents, elderly lawyers and spinster aunts of the fifty-year-old juveniles.

It was odd. It was often preposterous. But it was exciting. Here was some of the most wonderful production and acting you could wish for, just because the players and the audience were not confined in the strangling bonds of naturalism; they just had to use their imaginations, and use 'em plenty.

It was with a dull thud that we returned to the more commercially sophisticated theatre, to the smart alec playboys of the Western world, to temples whose high priests decreed that "young parts must be played by young people, fresh, pert, peppy, lively youngsters"; but where, thank God, the congregation has more sense. It realizes, as it has done from time immemorial, that youth has its place; but when it comes to a job of acting, of really getting to work on the minds and hearts and entrails of an audience, of really illuminating a text, of giving the works, then it would not exchange Miss Ruth Gordon, Miss Helen Hayes, Miss Lynn Fontanne, Messrs. Lunt, March, Tracy, Lahr and other old things in that approximate age-group, for twenty wildernesses of pert and peppy, lively, lovely, luscious but unaccomplished monkeys.

14. IF LOCAL THEATRE
IS TO PROSPER

ON A JULY EVENING more than a decade ago, Alec Guinness stepped onto the stage of the Shakespeare Festival Theatre at Stratford, Ontario, and began a performance of *Richard III*. The production marked the culmination of a year of extraordinary endeavor and vicissitudes. It also marked the establishment of a new and significant Canadian cultural institution. Canada has for many years publicly supported museums and art galleries, some symphony orchestras and an excellent public library system. But, until ten years ago, the professional theatre there was in poor shape and had received small public recognition and no public money.

It would be an exaggeration to say that the success of the Stratford Festival has created a full-fledged professional theatre in Canada. But it has made it possible for a group of Canadian actors and technicians to spend a sizable part of the year in interesting and serious theatrical work. It has raised both their wages and their status and enabled young people with a talent for the theatre to feel that there is a place for them at home, whereas a dozen or so years ago they had either to forego all hope of anything more ambitious than local church groups, or else go to London or New York with every likelihood of starvation or worse-than-death. The effect on the public is even more important, and to that we shall return shortly.

Meantime, let us consider the genesis of the Festival. Tom Patterson, a young Stratford journalist returning from war service in Europe, more particularly in Italy and London, was struck by the contrast between the quality and variety of entertainment in Europe and that available in his native city. The band concerts given by employes of the railway works were all very well; performances at the local Little Theatre were all very well; Old Home Week and the Annual Horse Show were all very well. But they were all artistically limited and all conducted on shoestring budgets. Patterson recalled the festival performances at Stratford-upon-Avon in Warwickshire. The town is a little smaller than Stratford, Ontario, a little sleepier, a great deal less affluent. He reckoned that what one little town had achieved the other might attempt.

To be sure, there existed no evidence that Shakespeare had been born in Stratford, Ontario; but the evidence in favor of that event having taken place in the Warwickshire Stratford is by no means incontrovertible—and anyway, what of it? The birthplace is no more than a gimmick, upon which hangs the promotion of Warwickshire's lucrative Shakespeare industry. What Warwickshire could do, Ontario could do with equal intelligence and idealism and more money.

No need to follow step by step as the enterprise emerged from dream to fact. Tom Patterson had the original impulse. His was the enthusiasm which eventually fired those who raised the money and took a long, anxious series of decisions and responsibilities. We can all build castles in Spain, hear harps in the air, create splendid imaginary festivals in our dull little city. Most of us never even attempt to transfer dream into fact; or, if we do, we give up after the first ten or twelve rebuffs. Patterson just refused to be rebuffed and it was due to his Scottish pertinacity that a climate of opinion began to form, a small body of citizens began to feel so strongly, even passionately, that, against all reasonable odds, they brought this Festival into being.

Facts. I will stick to what I know at first hand. I was invited to come from Ireland to give advice. Over the years I have done that to large numbers of bodies with admirable aims and eager enthusiasm. I thought I knew just what to expect: a dozen old women of both sexes, average age, sixty-eight. I could anticipate the setting of our meeting: the parlor of a rich widow in rimless glasses with blue hair; a delirium of central heat, African violets, a tiny, sickly dog and long-stemmed glasses of warm marsala.

The whole idea could not have been more wide of the mark.

The room was charming, the atmosphere businesslike, the committee quite young and obviously a cross-section. The males outnumbered the females five to one, but the women were handsome, spoke seldom and then to the point. Indeed, they were clearly no less in earnest, and rather more realistic, than the men.

All this was not an instantaneous impression. At first, because my fare had been paid by something called the Junior Chamber of Commerce, I was under the naïve impression that the aim of the enterprise was commercial. I therefore conceived it my duty to say that the production of Shakespeare was inevitably very expensive and not apt to be popular; that, in my opinion, it would pay better to hire a line of girls from New York and let them, to loud music and in a very bright light, kick about in what the crime reports call scanty attire.

I could feel the temperature in the room drop about forty degrees. Then spake the chairman: "I don't think you quite understand. We want to do something significant." In print that looks rather pompous, but his tone was anything but that. It was gentle and unassuming; yet behind it you could sense the faith which moves mountains.

By the end of that meeting—four hours later—we had agreed on the broad outline of the Festival and a large number of subsidiary details which, a year later, almost to the day, were embodied in that performance of *Richard III* in an amphitheatre covered by a gigantic canvas tent.

But, oh! between the cup and the lip how many slips, how many times the whole project teetered on the brink of disaster, the fringe of oblivion! I suppose that all ambitious projects are achieved by the few in the teeth not merely of apathy, but of the positive enmity, of the many, who are both timid and jealous. You can imagine, in a small, provincial town, what sniping took place from behind muslin curtains at a project, which was not only manifestly expensive but "long-haired"; which assumed that the cultural life of Stratford left something to be desired; which aimed to crowd the town with tourists, many of them dreadful, loud Americans; and worse, far worse, a project which was going to introduce into the community a lot of riff-raff, so called actors, the males at once bearded, effeminate and drunken, and the females—well, everyone knows what actresses are, just painted strumpets whose one idea is to show off.

I will not enlarge upon the difficulties—financial, social, moral and political. This is not because they were insignificant. Far from it. They were immense and, from time to time, seemed to be quite insurmountable. But difficulties have a way of melting, like snow in summer, under the sun of courageous, but reasonable, enthusiasm.

Were we fabulously lucky in Stratford? Or do there exist in a hundred small towns groups capable of a similar combination of vision, common sense and guts?

Anyway, eventually the money was raised and so was the tent. Many technical problems remained. The tent, owing to delay caused by repeated financial crises, arrived only at the eleventh hour. It was then discovered that it presented the inevitable acoustical difficulties. If you spoke quietly, you could not be heard at all; if you spoke loudly you sounded like five ogres roaring in a cave. There was a further phenomenon: sounds from the outer world were enormously magnified. Freight cars in the yards a mile away seemed to be shunting and banging right there in the tent. Mrs. A. on the next block would be talking quietly to her next-door neighbor, porch to porch, and there in the theatre, louder than the actors, you could hear a snip-by-snip description of her hysterectomy.

In the end, the opening passed off well. Women columnists were pleased with the audience's display of white dinner jackets, tartan cummerbunds, rubies, orchids, Dior gowns and long gloves. Dramatic critics were pleased with the talent of the company. Artistically and socially, the Festival had "arrived."

Naturally there were plenty to point out that although it had arrived it would not stay long. These people have been proved wrong. In its tenth summer the theatre played to an average of 94 per cent of its 2,000-seat capacity. During all preceding seasons attendance has never fallen to even three-quarters of capacity (the lowest was 77 per cent in 1957).

So much for quantity. What about quality? What sort of audience is this?

I have mentioned the social frou-frou of the first year's openings. Similar openings have persisted into other seasons—a splendid display of the Best People in the costliest cars and frocks. Now, while the Best People most certainly do not make the best audiences, they do make the headlines. A great deal of space in newspapers, and time on television, is occupied by the silliest gossip about who was there, what they wore and how elegantly metropolitan were the goings-on in an otherwise inconspicuous provincial town.

We must assume that editors are not completely out of touch with the tastes of their customers, that readers and viewers do, in fact, want this sort of gossip. Must we further assume that coverage of this sort, admittedly enormous, is good for a festival? Maybe it is. Maybe a large part of the audience is lured to a festival and unwillingly suffers the long boredom of a serious play in order to be part of the elegant goings-on which the mass media have glamorized.

Maybe. But, if it were so, I cannot believe that after opening nights the audiences would suddenly be *so* much less glamorous, and *so* much more alert. I must confine myself to Stratford, Ontario, because it is the only festival audience which I have observed closely; and it *is,* after opening nights, an alert audience, quick on the uptake, ready to be moved, ready to laugh, not timidly overawed or foolishly reverent before the performance of a great classic but, at the same time, intelligently respectful.

Where, I have heard it asked, is the summer festival audience in wintertime? Why is there such a rush to produce and see Shakespeare in the summer?

Well, in the first place, is there such a rush? Festivals have been inaugurated at Stratford, Connecticut; in New York City's Central Park (Mr. Papp's open-air theatre), in Ashland, Oregon, at Antioch College in Yellow Springs, Ohio, and in San Diego. There may be others, but I have not heard of them.

If there were even five others, would ten Shakespeare festivals in the whole of North America, none of them operated on anything but a moderate scale, constitute a remarkable boom in the production of work by the author who is generally acknowledged to be the greatest dramatic exponent of the English language?

In the second place, is it fair to imply that the organizers of such festivals are principally moved by love of gain, or their patrons by cultural snobbery? No one in possession of his five senses will maintain that producing Shakespeare is an easy way to make money. The plays cannot be got up without great expense; at the same time there is no reason to count on their drawing power at the box office, except when a celebrated actor has made a sensational success in one of the great roles. This is the principal reason why so little Shakespeare is seen in New York. No one can afford, at Broadway prices, to risk so costly an experiment, unless it is in some way underwritten. Mr. Sol Hurok has arranged Shakespeare seasons, underwritten by the celebrated name of the Old Vic; Mr. Papp's seasons, which are offered free, are supported by municipal and private funds. Neither method indicates that Shakespearean production is a gilt-edged investment.

Then are the organizers of the summer festivals catering just to cultural snobs?

There are people, not a few of them, who truly think that

if you express a preference for Leonardo over Norman Rock-well, for Bach over Gershwin, for Tolstoy over James Jones, that you simply cannot be sincere. There are others who, if you advance the notion that to enjoy Bach more than Gershwin demands a bit more musical education, as well as a bit more effort, will assert that your preference for Bach is a bare-faced and arrogant assertion of superiority over those less energetic or well-educated. I think there is an element of truth in this last accusation. But are we to be afraid to hold our own views, and indulge our own taste, simply because of a possible accusation of snobbery? Are we not to like cream simply because it is more expensive than skim milk? Surely cultural snobbery does not consist in preferring works of art which make more demand than more obviously popular works, but in pretending to do so for reasons of prestige.

Well, it may be that some of the summer festivals are organized by people who are only pretending to be interested. Again, I can only speak from experience. The promoters of the festival of Stratford, Ontario, have certainly impressed me by the sincerity of their interest, not just in their festival's success, but in the high and serious aims which its charter professes. Indeed, I cannot conceive of a group of people who would spend the time and energy which these people have upon their festival simply to be thought more clever and cultivated than they really are. But I can conceive of, indeed know, people, who, out of jealousy, make just such an accusation.

And what of the audiences? It is impossible to generalize. But I expect that at every serious theatrical occasion there are one or two people who are there because they think it is "the thing," rather than because they really expect to enjoy themselves. But I have never had the impression that the audience at Stratford, Ontario, had been hi-jacked by either social or cultural compulsion. It assembles in the simple-hearted and sensible expectation of enjoying itself; and, at the end, people come out looking as if that expectation has been fulfilled.

At Ashland, Oregon, the audience made a similar impression.

Most of us had traveled a considerable distance to get there; no one was elaborately dressed; the attention paid to the two performances which I saw was exemplary. The general effect was one of eager enjoyment to which the audience was itself an important contributor, not just a passive recipient. A snob audience does not, cannot, contribute in this way; it is timid, uncommitted, blasé.

In regard to this last, however, and in defense of fancy goings-on on opening nights, I think two things ought to be said. Negatively, they don't do much harm. I would not want to exchange the over-stuffed, but good-humored, condescension of the Best People for the over-intense scrutiny of an audience of well-informed enthusiasts. Neither one is representative of the public.

On the positive side, such frou-frou does create a sense of occasion. And this is one of the most valuable items in the stock-in-trade of the theatre. It is what television by its very nature finds hardest to achieve. It is what the movies have tried again and again to capture—without success.

All in all, I think that the theatre, even the so-called serious theatre, even theatrical festivals, do right to pander to the wish for glamorous, frivolous, garish opening nights. But how nice it would be if they were only reported on the Ladies Page; if the dramatic critics did not always have to attend this sort of occasion, but could see an ordinary performance sitting among ordinary human beings.

Meanwhile, let us welcome the emergence of the theatre festival. We had better face the fact that road companies are on their very last legs. Tours no longer make sense artistically or economically. It is still possible for managements to make a profit out of touring cast-iron successes, like *My Fair Lady,* while the reverberation of their Broadway successes is still in the air, but that is about all. And it would be idle to pretend that the touring version can be as good as the original. The cast may be no less talented, the scenery and dresses may be exact reproductions of the original; still, the fact remains that what results is a warmed-up helping of cold pudding. And the further fact remains that, after a month or two of touring, cast, scenery, dresses and everything else simply cannot but have a jaded air. What Kansas City and Seattle see are the flowers of Tuesday's dinner table at breakfast on Saturday.

For Kansas City, and Seattle, and half a hundred other cities, the festival is the answer, if they want a live theatre. Let them organize it for themselves and create the sort of event which they themselves want and which suits their own locality. It will not be easy, but the difficulties are not insuperable. Money *can* be raised; practical plans *can* be evolved; artists *can,* rather easily, be persuaded to leave New York and go to the ends of the earth, if they are persuaded that at the ends of the earth an interesting job awaits them. And, finally, there *is* a public, which is literally dying of starvation—not for culture with a capital C, but for something which they believe is worth the alert, energetic attention of a grown-up person.

I believe this to be true because I have been closely connected with two such festivals. Stratford, Ontario, is now a strongly entrenched institution, the recipient of both federal and provincial subsidy, a respected symbol of the gradual emergence of Canada from one stage of development to another, not better, but more mature and sophisticated.

Minneapolis still is an infant festival, but indications are strong that the infant will thrive. The first moves have been made. After three years of preparatory work, the money was collected, a building created, a company of actors gathered. Indications are that for such a theatre, making no attempt to be popular in the sense of condescending to a public which is presumed incapable of serious effort, there will always be a solid and loyal following.

I think that the organizers of a dramatic festival must assume that there exists a public whose taste the mass-distributive media underestimate. I see no point in duplicating the standard popular program which the movies and television are already offering. There is evidence of the existence of a public hungry for something better—and sufficiently numerous to make a better program economically and artistically viable.

Pending a more accurate definition, I suggest that a better program be founded upon classical works, that is to say, works about whose merit the best minds have been agreed for several generations. The analogy of music may be useful here. Any symphony orchestra bases its program upon the work of generally agreed masters—Bach, Mozart, Beethoven, Brahms. These will not exclusively provide the program; but they are the foundation; it is through their performance that both the taste of the public and the technique of the players is principally developed. Analogously, only by performance of the great dramatic classics can a theatre company be trained and a standard of criticism be developed by the audience.

A person who has no training or experience can no more be a wise critic of drama than of music or painting or, for that matter, of politics or baseball. This would seem to be a truism, but I think it is a general assumption that anyone—literally anyone—can open his mouth and pass judgment on a theatrical performance, whether of *Oedipus Rex* or *Abie's Irish Rose*. Naturally, everyone is entitled to an opinion; but not everyone is entitled to have his opinion taken seriously.

If a theatre is to prosper, not just materially but as an expression of a community, it must create a rapport between its performances and its audience; to this end the audience must not only be collected, but, further, instructed. Only thus can a mutually fruitful relation be established between artist and public. In other arts this is recognized. In the theatre, because in this country it is organized and predominantly regarded not as an art but a business, the theatrical artist is considered a mere salesman whose public is his customer. It then follows that he must strive to please customers, most of whom are quite ignorant and quite humbly and gently aware of their ignorance in this particular field.

It is even sillier in art than in business to pretend that the customer is always right; even to pretend that the customer always knows what he wants. He wants what he can be persuaded to want; and the artist who regards himself as no more than a supplier of what the public thinks it wants is taking an inadequate view of his own social responsibility.

If the theatre is to survive—and I do not imply the slightest doubt of its survival—it can only be as something more serious and interesting than showbiz. Showbiz can be fun, exciting, delightful—and financially profitable. But insofar as it is organized only as a business, whose first duty is to make a profit for the shareholders, the aim is fatally limited. The theatre must exist to serve the public, to fill an imaginative void, to feed the appetite, the enormous appetite, of the human creature for dramatic fiction.

This presupposes some responsibility—maybe not even that, maybe no more than common sense—on the part of both feeders and fed, in order that the diet be both agreeable and nourishing.

15. ADIEU, "OLD" MET!

NEW PRODUCTIONS at the Metropolitan Opera each year remind us what an undertaking a great opera company is. What an infinity of planning and contriving, what a heap of talent, technique and just plain pulling and heaving is involved! It's a pretty considerable cope in Bayreuth or Milan, where the opera season is the main social and artistic event of the year, one of the mainsprings of community life, and where, consequently, the wheels of production are oiled by public money and, no less important, public understanding and prestige. It's an even greater cope in London or Paris, where the prestige of opera is less, where the public subsidies are smaller, where the opera is competing as one of many theatrical attractions, and where most of the operatic repertoire is not native, but exotic—a great, sickly, waxy flower, in most cases already overblown.

In New York the case is harder still. The flower of nine-teenth-century grand opera—and, with due respect to the fact that a brand new work is very occasionally produced, the Met's repertoire has hardly changed in sixty years—is even more exotic here than in London or Paris, and even more overblown; the competition with other entertainments is no less fierce; there is no public subsidy whatever; and the costs of produc-tion, owing to the very much higher wages paid to everyone from diva to call boy, are, by European standards, gargantuan. The result is that the opera house is only maintained by the subscriptions of wealthy well-wishers. Inevitably these people tend to be elderly or, if not elderly, at least of very conservative outlook. Their taste, fairly enough, is reflected in the program which they subsidize.

Thus we have the odd paradox that of all the great opera houses, the Met is, in most of the ways that matter, the most old-fashioned, the nearest to the theatre of our grandparents, and even of their parents. This even extends to the audience. Nowhere else in the world has such an audience survived. It is one of the great charms of New York that at the Met one may still see bejeweled *grandes dames,* rouged like crazy, wearing what at first glance appear to be black fur stoles, but what turn out to be their enervated sons slung across mama's magnificent shoulders. One may still see elderly patricians hanging from their boxes by the heels, with their opera glasses pointing like guns right down the bosom of a huge soprano. One may still see swarms of liveried chauffeurs waiting to escort their employers to their cars, to place fur wraps about their aged shanks, to touch their caps respectfully at the words, "Home, James and don't spare the Packard."

Backstage, at the "old" Met—it is too early to say what things will be like at the new building—an old world charm prevails which makes Broadway seem remote indeed. Functionaries from Nebraska call other functionaries from Idaho not "Hank" or "Mr. Schultz," but "Maestro." The stage manager wears faultless evening dress and a crimson carnation. The property master wears a checkered cap and looks like a character part out of Dickens—no, early Priestley. There are endless iron staircases with choristers coming and going, dressed for balls in Vienna, as grisettes or huntsmen; there are nooks and corners full of wigs and top boots and rose pink chiffon; there are pianos everywhere—even in the washrooms—and at the pianos are creatures called *répétiteurs,* whose duty it is to pound the music into the skulls of the singers. Everywhere, everywhere is heard the din of practice, a cacophony of glorious voices pouring forth in unrelated, meaningless cascades.

Here is a dressing room marked "Tenori." There is a crimson carpet, worn and stained, but the wreck of a good carpet. The furniture is good old stuff. This is not the rickety, rackety rubbish provided in the dressing rooms on Broadway. It is stiflingly hot, because we have shut the door—heavy mahogany— to keep out the din of practice. Before a gold-framed cheval-glass —a real "piece"—a plump little gentleman, heavily rouged and in a ginger wig, is surveying his reflection through thick spectacles. He is dressed as a Highland chieftain, but the kilt hanging well below his knees gives him the air of a female impersonator. The ginger wig is surmounted by a jaunty Highland bonnet, black velvet with a great black feather. About his person is disposed a staggering assortment of Scottish bijouterie— plaids, dirks, sporrans, cairngorms. In high-heeled patent pumps he stands every inch of five feet. "Like it?" he asks in tones of liquid gold, "I designed it myself." A tap on the mahogany door: "Overture, Beginners," cries a voice. "Purrd'n me," says the Highland chief and, removing his glasses, teeters toward the stage.

On with the motley. The show must go on. And, somehow, night after night at the Met the show does go on.

No one, except those who have been through it, can believe the flurry, the fuss, the frenzy involved in the production of a Broadway musical. It's hard to know quite why this should be so, perhaps it is because of the way that money is regarded. Every season literally millions of dollars are collected to produce musical comedies. Most of it is subscribed by people who have no artistic interest whatever. They don't ask to read the script, or to hear a score. They are merely speculators. If the production is a hit, they will make several hundred percent. If, as is considerably more likely, it is a flop, their loss is tax deductible. Now, somehow, once this money, so frivolously subscribed, passes into the care of the producer, it seems—and I guess this is a tribute to his probity—to acquire a semi-sacred significance. Henceforth it is referred to as The Investment. There is a great deal of anxious talk about protecting The Investment, and, from this point on until the production, which The Investment exists to create, reaches the stage, no one makes any decision alone. Everything, from important matters like casting, down to trifles like the color of the shoes which the chorus men will wear in the garden scene—everything has to be the subject of a conference, involving the producer, the designer, the director, and probably another half-dozen persons, possibly including an author or composer, with a secretary to take notes, another to fetch coffee, and a third because she is so pretty. The object of these conferences is to protect The Investment from foolish or precipitate decisions.

Naturally, the agreements thus reached represent what nobody very much cares about rather than what anybody very much wants. Agreements of this character may do in politics, but they certainly don't produce works of art. The frustrating consciousness of this, the boredom and nervous strain of the conferences, screws all the participants into a tight knot of neurotic tension. This, naturally, expresses itself in their work. The rot spreads downward to the lower echelons. There are screams at rehearsals, scenes at the costumer's, chorus boys take the vapors, bassoon players beat their wives, promising careers are ruined. During the try-outs authors destroy themselves in Wilmington, in New Haven, and in dozens. The whole thing turns out to be an unparalleled disaster. But honor has been satisfied. The producer has bust a gut to protect The Investment.

Obviously at the Met there is a pretty big investment too. The opera house employs an orchestra rather more than three times greater than would, in musical comedy, be considered a large ensemble. The chorus is about five times as large. There is, in addition, a great corps of principal artists, many of them of international renown, few of whom sing more than three times in a fortnight. After the production of a Broadway musical, its producers sink back exhausted and gasping. One production in a season seems like hard work. The Met expects to maintain a repertoire of twenty to twenty-four operas; that means not only that the scenery and costumes are available, but that these works are rehearsed. In addition, the repertoire each season includes four or five new productions. At the Met, three complete stage crews each work an eight-hour shift throughout every twenty-four hours of every day of the working week.

Thus, when the show goes on at the Met, not only is a good deal of effort involved, but, in order to preserve the sanity, even the very lives, of those principally concerned, there is a good deal more organization, discipline and horsesense than is usually available to protect The Investment.

My own connection with the Met has been as a stage director. Until comparatively recently, directors, in what is euphemistically referred to as "the straight" or "the legitimate" theatre, did not get invited to work in opera. But at the Met Mr. Rudolf Bing, the General Manager, has had the new productions staged by people whose experience has not been confined to opera houses and whose work is thought to be contemporary. The same thing is happening all over the world. It is realized that opera cannot stand still, that we cannot indefinitely accept productions in the style of fifty or sixty years ago. It is not that modern productions are better, but there are fashions in all departments of human expression, just as in dress. The conventions and fashions of theatrical production change slowly but inexorably, so that a production of 1900 now looks just as démodé as the clothes of 1900. But to say this implies neither censure of the by-gone nor praise of the modern mode.

The great problem of staging an opera in the conditions which apply to all the great opera houses, except Bayreuth and Glyndebourne, is shortage of time. At the Met, for *La Traviata*, we worked under optimum conditions. This opera is not only a masterpiece, but a war-horse. Mr. Bing hoped, therefore, that this production might be available for many years—perhaps for a decade. The principals were a galaxy of stars, the scenery and dresses were entrusted to artists of top reputation, no reasonable expense was grudged, and, during the period of rehearsal we had top priority in the Met's bewilderingly complex schedule. In fact, however, all this only amounted to the equivalent of five hours of rehearsal time for each act. Since two of the acts required complicated ensemble maneuvers by over a hundred people, most of the time had to be spent on these. All that I or, I venture to think, any other director could possibly achieve was a reasonably efficient job of traffic direction. There was no time to do anything like discuss the nature of the work we were attempting to stage, to consider whether our various interpretations might not be brought into rather closer cohesion, both in technique and intention, than in fact they were. The eminent principals had performed their roles many, many times in many different productions in many parts of the world. I had directed the work several times before. We all had our ideas. I didn't like some of theirs, and I'm sure they didn't like a lot of mine. But there was good will and, given time, I think we might have achieved a real collaboration. Something interesting might possibly have emerged, something which would make this great masterpiece speak again in terms of theatre, not just as a series of great melodies. But there was no time; and the opera went on, looking handsome, splendidly sung, but not interpreted theatrically at all.

I think if opera is to survive, ways will have to be contrived to give enough time for the reconsideration of the established masterpieces. Without such reconsideration they grow lifeless and stale. The purely musical meaning does undergo a continuous process of careful and expert re-examination by conductors and *répétiteurs*. For the acting side of the work there is no comparable preparation. Moreover the artists are not engaged as actors, but as singers. It has not been God's plan always to place the finest voices in the most beautiful bodies, nor to make them the instruments of the liveliest minds. Nor is it considered necessary that an opera singer should be an educated or cultivated person. Many of them are, but so are many taxi drivers. It is not regarded as an indispensable qualification for either job.

Comparatively few singers would see the least point in reconsidering the dramatic interpretation of the works to which their careers are dedicated. How could they reconsider what they have never considered in the first place? For the most part singers are content to stand where they are placed, to move when and whither they are requested, and in between what they call "the actions" to face front, watch the beat, and sing the role according to the guidance of their *répétiteur*. The stage director to them is a tedious and irrelevant fusspot, who comes between them and the music. I suspect that this is an attitude which they share with most of the professional critics of opera. There is the feeling that the singers, certainly, and a large majority of their audience, probably, would prefer their opera in concert versions—singers in evening dress standing in a row in front of organ pipes, chorus piled up on bleachers behind them—the good old lay-out, hallowed by oratorio.

Yet, if that was what they wanted, Verdi, Wagner, Puccini and the rest of them could so easily have indicated their wish. But, clearly, no. They intended their works to be not merely sung but also acted.

What a glorious thing a really great performance of opera can be! It occurs only very, very rarely. Performances at the Met and Covent Garden, in Paris, Berlin, Dresden, Milan, Stockholm, and everywhere else are frequently feeble and dreary and sometimes ridiculous. That's the price which has to be paid for attempting something so difficult, and just barely possible—something which rarely, but still occasionally, can be sublime.

I suggest that the Met might be sublime more often than it is, if two reforms could be effected. Neither of them lies within the power of the management alone; both demand the cooperation of the general public and, most of all, of the wealthy patrons. The first would be to put on fewer productions in a season. This would give more time for preparation. It would mean that certain works would be performed more frequently in a given season. It is my contention that better prepared performances would attract a very much wider audience. The second reform lies almost entirely in the hands of the public. It is this: At present more interest is focused on great performers than upon either the works in which they appear, or the ensemble which surrounds them. This means that the predominant aim of the Met is, by public demand, to acquire great voices, rather than to present a distinguished ensemble. This leads to vulgarities like the pitting of one artist against another, each patently supported by a claque, and to excessive ovations for individuals.

But these are comparatively minor points. The fact remains that the Met is one of the great opera houses of the world. In New York it is almost the only professional theatrical venture which is conducted with a long-term plan and an artistic policy, which is not just a speculation but a public institution, where respectability is matched with brilliance, where, over the years, there begins to be formed a tradition.

It is sad to think that the beautiful old opera house has just about run its course. But, when the Met moves uptown, with the truckloads of scenery, the mountain of boots and feathers and halberds, the goblets, rosaries, banners and fans, something will also move uptown, invisible, intangible, inaudible, but stronger than tried steel: the tradition which only forms around a collective activity which has been going on for many years. It is the sum of many people's long sustained effort, distilled of blood and sweat and tears. Alone, of all New York's theatrical enterprises, the Met has it. It is more precious than rubies.

16. OTHER PUBLIC PLEASURES

Football at Manchester

These are descriptions of five non-theatrical entertainments seen from the point of view of a theatrical director. Association football is probably the most popular sport in England. This particular game took place in Manchester, a vast, black city in the North of England, the center of Lancashire's textile industry.

It was a mid-week match and didn't begin till a quarter past six. People went to it straight from work. There was a splendid service of special busses—a ceaseless stream, with kind, fatherly inspectors laid on to load us up and pile us in. But even so, it took twenty-five minutes to work from the tail to the head of the line. We were an overwhelming majority of men—seventy, I should reckon, to one woman—most of us in work clothes, dungarees predominant.

It was a fine evening, but cold—distinctly nippy—with the pearly light of April on the great black warehouses. There wasn't much talk. Most people read the evening paper: thousands of men patiently standing in line, patiently sucking the mental dope provided by the press barons—Russia, Czechoslovakia, Blue Baby in Oxygen Tent; Russia, Margaret Lockwood, Bantu Minstrel Wins Again; Russia, Czechoslovakia, A New Way with Hake Fritters; Russia. . . .

We were a "capacity gate," seventy-two thousand of us. Looking across to the other side of the field, the people opposite appeared like a colossal oblong of pink sago pudding—each grain of sago being a human face, a real face like yours and mine, two eyes, a nose and other appropriate external fittings, and, inside, presumably impulses and ideas and all that. Beyond and above the heads were the roofs and chimneys of rows and rows of suburban houses. And beyond the houses a great black church spire—Victorian-Gothic heavenward gesture—and beyond that a glimpse of the Pennine Hills in the pearly light; and beyond that a great towering mass of gray clouds, edged with apricot jam.

By now the silence had changed to an enormous hum. And suddenly the hum became a roar, a great beast's yell. The teams had appeared, from a sort of underground cavity. They ran up and out onto the turf that looked so artificial, surrounded by its seventy-two thousand grains of sago—Manchester United in blue jerseys, Manchester City in red. Or were United red and City blue? What does it matter?

I am not going to attempt to describe the match. I am not qualified to do so. I want instead to convey to you, if I can, how it struck me as a drama. I think it is reasonable for someone with my professional background and training to look at other activities in terms of drama, just as it would be reasonable for an anthropologist to attend a funeral in a rather more analytic spirit than the average guest's, and to draw inevitable comparisons with similar rites in other epochs and other communities; or just as it would be reasonable for a clergyman to go to the theatre and see in the rites there performed the worship of a god, or maybe of gods.

But back to Manchester and the match.

From the moment the game began the great crowd sprang into violent and corporate life. Not, of course, that we were unanimous: some of us were fanatical in support of City, some no less so for United, some were neutral. But we were all focused on the same event, and shared the same excitement. We were one beast, divided—like any other beast—by conflicting reactions, conflicting impulses but none the less one.

On the whole we were a gentle beast. Compared, for instance, with a baseball crowd in New York, or an ice-hockey crowd in Montreal, we weren't very bloodthirsty. There was no barracking, no furious exhortations of the players to violence, no vicious cursing of incompetents. I remember once, in Montreal, how a hockey player who made a bad mistake was pelted by the audience with their overshoes. The air was dark with hundreds of flying galoshes, and truly frightful streams of objurgation.

But this was not Quebec, this was Lancashire, where a century of life in overcrowded industrial towns has conditioned people to an almost saintly patience with one another. Manners here may not be of metropolitan elegance, but they are very, very kind. We mooed and booed when we suspected foul play, we yelled and bawled our approval of good play. I suppose most of the noise we made must be described as aggressive, when the stimulus is—as this was, as all games are—a mimic battle. And isn't this rather a good way to get aggressive impulses off one's chest? Better anyway than bear-baiting, bull fighting, fox hunting, or the shooting of driven birds. The animals who were performing for us were paid to do so, and were in no grave risk of death. Incidentally, to an ignoramus like myself, their skill and speed were most impressive and beautiful.

I don't think there is anything in Association Football as aesthetically satisfying as a good three-quarter movement in Rugby, but all in all it did make a very fine spectacle. I was struck, as often before, by the similarity between these ball-games and ballet. Both depend upon the deployment of a group of figures into a conventionally prescribed space. In the case of ballet, rhythm is supplied by the beat of the music; in games, by the movement of the ball. But in both, the movement of the figures, both individually and collectively, is a reaction to the rhythmic impulse of music or ball.

Also, as in ballet, it is clear that one of the great attractions of football is the magnetism of its stars. To me, the great distance between the players and myself was a considerable handicap to any appreciation of individual performances or individual personalities. Unfamiliar spectator as I am, I found myself watching just a group of remote red and blue midgets, just—but only just—distinguishable one from t'other by the color of their hair. But to everyone else they seemed to be familiar public personalities: Stan and Tommy, and old Wilfred. Gossip was exchanged about their exploits and careers and mannerisms; their form was minutely criticized.

Indeed, it is obvious that this element of personality, or hero-worship of star magnetism is one of the great attractions of the game. And that being so, I find it odd that, in a sport so frankly commercialized, it is not more exploited. I find it odd that the whole spectacle is presented with so little showmanship. The ground is so bleak and ugly—just banks of cement with a few dingy advertisements urging one to buy this tobacco, that beer. And at half-time, at the beginning and the end, a cluster of iron lilies brayed out recorded voluntaries so halfheartedly, with such absolute absence of joy. I wonder whether the instinct which impels the fans to bring rattles and twirl them like corn crakes in the mating season, the instinct which expresses itself in rosettes and paper hats in club colors—whether this impulse toward color and music should not be more cultivated and encouraged, and whether the whole affair would be more fun if it was more gay. And yet . . . and yet, in that gray twilight in the Manchester suburbs, wouldn't gaiety have been absurdly out of place and insultingly synthetic? I don't think our native British idea of a good time necessarily includes gaiety. And we *did* have a good time. It was madly exciting. It was grand.

Side by side with the mimic battle of the match, I thought I could feel another, perhaps more significant, battle taking place, unconsciously. A conflict between the separate identity of each one of us—with his private impulses, private repressions, his own individual standards of propriety and conventions of good behavior—and the great uninhibited, unintellectual, unrespectable, roaring, yelling, carefree crowd-beast into which all our identities were partly fused. Partly, not altogether: the

collective and the individual soul were fighting, like the red
team and the blue, for mastery.

I think my impression of the audience is best crystallized by
the pair right behind me—a father and son. The father was a
gentle, worn-out looking man, in dungaree trousers under a
black overcoat; the son was a stoutish youth of about eight,
called, as I afterward learned, Herbert. They shared a paper
screw of licorice allsorts in impenetrable silence, a silence broken
but twice. Once, when Manchester United had the narrowest of
squeaks, disaster averted only by a heroic piece of goal-keeping
—once, just this once, young Herbert uttered a single, piercing
scream that must have been audible in Peru. His soul flew
out of his mouth with a sound like a fiend in torment. I glanced
round and saw his little pudding face transfigured; his cheeks
were as red as fire and his eyes were blazing like twin stars.
Then the pair were silent again till the end of the game. The
whistle had blown, the red team and the blue had left the field,
twilight was falling, and so was a mizzle of April rain, the great
composite crowd-monster was breaking up into seventy-two
thousand separate particles. There was a deep, deep sigh from
Herbert, whether of despair or contentment will never be
known, for all he said was, "Eh, Dad." And the father said,
"Aye, that's that." Then he took the little boy's hand, and
said, "Coom, 'Erbert."

We all wandered out into the streets—docile, separate, tiny
identities again—to find the twilight had deepened into dusk.
Street lamps were on, turning us all into livid, arsenical green
ghosts. There was a lighted window, and on its sill three tiny
little girls in white nightdresses had been allowed to sit up
to see the crowds go past. There was a figure in shirt sleeves
who called out from a dark doorway, "Puss, Puss, Puss," and
then, to no one in particular, "Who won?" And a dozen voices
answered from the dusk, "No one, it was a draw." And bus
after bus after bus after lighted bus went back to town, loaded
with silent sportsmen, whose heads were bowed over evening
papers—Russia, Czechoslovakia, Margaret Lockwood, Bantu

Minstrel, and Hake Fritters. "Who won?" No one. It was a
draw.

Brass Bands at Bolton

Lancashire and Yorkshire are the centers of Britain's cotton
and wool industries. There are large numbers of manufacturing
towns which to an outsider might seem painfully ugly, unculti-
vated, rough, but when you get to know them better you find
beneath the somewhat unglamorous surface great richness of
character and depth of feeling. This expresses itself to a considerable extent in music. The Huddersfield Choral Society is
world-famous, but there are a dozen great choirs. There also
exists a great popular tradition of instrumental playing. In all
the big cities and many quite small areas there will be a number
of brass bands. Most of the big firms run their own bands and
rivalry between them is keen. There is a National Brass Band
Association which organizes competitions in different areas
of the country. I attended one such competition at Bolton.

Bolton is a cotton town in Lancashire, not far from Manchester. It is a very large town, but in most respects a very
provincial, undistinguished wilderness of liver-colored brick.

The contest began at one.

An hour before that the teams had met for the draw, to
decide in which order they must play.

This is important. A good band seems even better if it
follows a poor one. So the order cannot be decided by the
management, it must be left to the luck of the draw. It's fairer
so.

Immense care is taken to make the contest impartial. The
judges are not allowed to know which team is playing, in case
they should be unconsciously influenced by the *beaux yeux* of
the bandsmen or the reputation of the conductor. They are so
placed that they can hear but not see. They spend the afternoon, poor things, locked in a sort of dog-kennel—a crate with

a small hole at the top for air. They did come out alive. I saw
them.

But I anticipate.

At one o'clock sharp I was at the Victoria Hall, Bolton.
Today its entrance hall is like the Court of Ruritania: scores
of men in spanking pseudo-military uniforms—scarlet, maroon,
royal blue and emerald, set off, as they say, by gold braid and
a heartening flourish of silver euphoniums, cornets and trombones. Like Cardinal Newman, "I loved the garish day, and
spite of fears, Pride ruled my will," and I thrust through the
Lancers, Grenadiers, Marines and Hussars to the box office.

Alas, the illusion of Ruritania was but fleeting. The Victoria
Hall, Bolton, is not a bit like the Royal Palace at Strelsau.
It is a dingy mid-Victorian public building with a platform,
galleries and piercing drafts, and in the middle—virgin white
amid the encircling gloom—the judges' box, crate, kennel,
cubby or den.

At one o'clock there was but a sprinkling of us present. For
at one we were only to hear the Fourth Division contest. It is
rather like football. The first and second teams in this year's
Fourth Division can go up next year into the Third. And so
on season by season to the top—or championship—class. The
Top Division Contest wasn't until four o'clock.

I should explain that this was an Area Qualifying Contest.
Winners and seconds of each division here will compete at a
National Contest in October at the Albert Hall, in London.
So great is the interest in this National Contest that, in the
past, as many as thirty thousand people have applied for tickets.
Of course, compared to figures of football, dog-racing, or movie
attendance, thirty thousand is a mere fleabite. But one cannot
estimate significance by statistics alone. Football is a much
easier event to follow than a band contest. It demands far less
concentration, far less previous knowledge, and its thrill is far
more primitive. I have no doubt that on the same analogy, if
some modern Lady Godiva were to announce her act at Coven-
try, or if a public execution, or even a good flogging were

to be advertised, the application for tickets would exceed the wildest dreams of modern sport promotion.

One must not confuse the quality of a spectacle with its popularity. I must confess that I had no idea brass band contests were as popular as they are. And now that I've been to one, I'm still surprised. Not that it wasn't first-class entertainment; it was. But it's quite difficult entertainment. I don't think the casual visitor would enjoy it very much. And I don't think in this audience there were many casual visitors. We were either supporters of the various competing teams, a lot of whom had traveled considerable distances, or else pretty expertly qualified observers. I made friends with one of these latter. When I arrived, there were still plenty of empty seats, so, as I knew so little about it all and wanted to ask a lot of questions, I picked a friendly-looking neighbor.

Let me tell a little about him, because I think he epitomizes this audience.

He lives near Wigan, not very far from Bolton, works as a laborer in a paint factory. He used to be a coal miner but his pit closed down due to flooding. He plays the cornet in a local band, but, so he said, his band is not up to contest standard. Not even the Fourth Division. None the less he knows plenty about the brass band business. He knew all the principal personalities—conductors and players—and entertained me greatly with gossip about them. He was a highly intelligent critic of technique and taught me some of the things to listen for, some of the elements of brass band appreciation. And he had a fine sense of the relation between technique and interpretation. In other words, he knew his onions. I had made a lucky shot in sitting next to him.

And that's the whole point. I could have picked lots of others no less qualified to instruct and inform, though none could have been more friendly and cordial. There were dozens of men like him there, people with no pretensions whatever about being musicians or critics or intelligentsia and what-have-you, but who knew plenty about what they were listening to, and could talk about it well. It was an exceedingly intelligent, expert, alert audience. The occasion, consequently, was most stimulating.

What about the performance?

Ah! There I'm not going to commit myself. I don't know enough about it. I only know that some of the Fourth Division bands gave me great pleasure. But my companion was merciless in his kind dismissal: "It's nice for them," he would say, "to have the experience. They'll enjoy the outing. But this isn't brass band playing. Wait for the Championship."

Well, of course he was right.

The Fourth Division had played three little pieces—quite pretty and by no means, or so I thought, too childishly easy. The Champions, however, played a fantasia of airs by Mozart, arranged for brass by Sir Malcolm Sargent. And arranged, I suspect, by this master showman to provide every test of skill. There were great massive held chords, and rapid runs and counterpoint, and an adagio theme that was a trap to all but the top conductors. The less sophisticated bands let it degenerate into a bit of a wallow, like the Salvation Army letting its hair down over a juicy six-eight hymn. Only the top men retained a classic dignity and style. Then, toward the end, there was a cadenza for solo cornet, winding up with a trill in which he was joined first in thirds by a second soloist, then by all the cornets, then by all the band. No! I don't think the trombones were expected to do it—I'm not sure—but certainly great fat euphoniums were trilling away like mad.

By four o'clock the hall had filled up. People had been flowing in steadily all afternoon, and expectation was all agog. A really wonderful atmosphere. As good luck would have it, the team drawn to play first in the Championship Class was the celebrated band of the Fairey Aviation Works under a star conductor. Suddenly one heard what brass band playing could be. The brilliance, and at the same time the sweetness and expressiveness of the tone fairly lifted one out of Bolton's Victoria Hall, half way to heaven. My friend just gave me a wink to imply, "What did I tell you!" He was too critically attentive to do more.

The Fairey crowd were good, marvelously good. But they only got second place! We placed them second as well as the judges. But the team we had spotted as winners—Manchester Co-op—only came fourth. The judges gave top to Wingates Temperance. Well . . . certainly Wingates were pretty hot stuff and I suppose the judges knew their business. . . . But what an afternoon those judges had—locked for five hours in a crate in the Victoria Hall.

And what a good idea of someone's this contest is. These are the objectives for which it was founded, the championship I mean, and I quote a leaflet:

1. To continue the splendid traditions of the Crystal Palace Championship festivals, which were held from 1900–1938.
2. To foster improvements in contesting conditions throughout the country.
3. To make the greatest possible contribution to the development of brass instrumental music.

These brass bands are one of the comparatively few cultural by-products of industry. From a solely musical point of view, a brass band, exciting as is the noise it makes, is rather a limited instrument of expression. But, taking a wider view of art, this brass band tradition and the attitude to recreation which this contest at Bolton expresses, are highly significant and valuable.

As sporting events go, this was a small event numerically. But significance and value—one cannot remember this too often —simply cannot be assessed in terms of figures at the box office, reckoned by clocks in a turnstile. Quantity is one thing, quality another. Quantity is often positively inimical to quality. One of the dangers in a society that is trying, as ours is, to be equalitarian, is that activities tend to be thought of as important simply because they are popular. And, what is more sinister, what gives the lie to the equalitarian pretensions of such thoughts, is that popular activities are apt to be confounded with valuable activities for no better reason than that their promotion pays a fat dividend.

Going to the Dogs

A different kind of relation exists between performers and audience at another entertainment popular in the British Isles —greyhound racing. Not long ago I went to the dogs at the Bellevue track in Manchester.

There was a big crowd. I'm no good at estimating figures, but there were many thousands present, and the Tote indicated that thousands of pounds changed hands at every race. During the evening there were six races. Each race takes but a minute or two, then there's a twenty minute interval. You might suppose, as I did at first, that the proportion of interval compared to racing was rather high. But that, I think, is to misunderstand the point. The racing certainly goes on, but the business which is transacted between the races—well, that goes on too and is very absorbing.

First let me try to give you some picture of what it looks like: a great oval arena of green turf in the center, cinder-covered banks all round, and two grandstands. One of these stands is just part of the ordinary accommodation; the other is grander—double entrance money—and commands the best view of the winning post. In this grandstand is the judge's box; and there's a specially select bit, partitioned off by walls of glass, reserved for committee members and their friends. One can peer at them through the glass wall and they look like goldfish in a tank, only perhaps not quite so decorative. And, like goldfish, they seem to spend a lot of their time consuming light refreshments.

The dogs, of course, run round the perimeter of the oval greensward following the course of the little tramline upon which runs the electric hare. More of this later.

It was a cold evening, just beginning to be twilight. During the course of a race the track is lit by powerful lamps on concrete standards—rather nice, like the lighting of a railway shunting yard. Between races, no doubt from motives of laudable economy, these lights are switched off. The whole scene is twilit, cigarette butts glow, all faces are in shadow, except the great many-clocked face of the Tote. That is all right. The whole scene is dominated by this enormous Totalizator or Tote. It looks like a gigantic scoreboard, and shows you at a glance which race is on, and on six clockfaces what are the odds at each particular second on each of the six dogs taking part. Don't ask me how the Tote works. I am told it costs £70,000 (about $200,000) to make, and that a staff of highly-paid experts is required to operate it. Hardly surprising. The blooming thing can practically talk!

There are booking offices all over the ground; wherever you may be, you don't have to walk far to lay your money. They are just like ordinary booking offices in a railway station or movie theatre—a hole in a wooden partition and, sitting behind the hole, a very pleasant and patient lady, who takes your money and issues an appropriate ticket. Then, after the race, you go back to a similar window and, if you've won, a similar lady gives you the appropriate sum of money. She's connected by electricity with the wonderful Tote and it tells her, just as it tells everyone else, how much is due. If you've lost, naturally you don't bother going back to the window, because of course your money's already inside there.

I must go on a bit about the ladies inside the windows. Sheltered blossom that I am, I had never before been to the dogs and, I think, unconsciously expected to meet a lot of loud-voiced, foul-oathed, gin-sodden character-parts from films and novels. I was half prepared to be clunked on the head with a bottle, even slashed with a razor. I was a little (such is the

perversity of human nature) disappointed to find the whole
affair to be conducted with the decorum of a Sunday School
and these ladies in the boxes, instead of being the sinful ogresses
of my bourgeois imagination, were fresh-faced things in beau-
tifully clean pinafores who said "Ta, Love," when they gave
change and "Bye Bye for now." They were simply sweet when
ignoramuses, like myself, who didn't know their way about the
maze of slang and technical terms employed by the experienced
punters—One and Two, Win and Place, Straight Forecast, and
a hundred-and-fifty other expressions that were Greek to me.
Not that it's very difficult. The windows are labeled with different monetary figures—2/–, 4/–, 10/–, and £1—you'd be
amazed at the number and kind of people who plonk down quite
large sums without moulting a feather. (One pound is about
$2.80; one shilling is 14¢.)

I went naturally to the cheapest, the two bob window, and
very shyly muttered the very silly name of the dog I fancied.
"Win or Win-and-Place, dear?" said the lady, and when I
goggled she explained very kindly, as to a small child, what
she meant. No one in the long queue behind me gave sound or
hint that this delay was a bore. I've forgotten already what it all
meant. I only know that I had to cough up four shillings and
got in return two tickets, one of which was useless and the other
of which I was later able to exchange for eight shillings. It
sounds easy, doesn't it? But of course sometimes you don't win.
And the shaming thing is that when you do win, even by the
merest fluke like this, you can't help feeling pleased and proud
and clever.

I went with two friends as silly and ignorant as myself, and
between us we made money. Not a lot, not quite enough to
recoup the price of our entrance (it's quite expensive to get
in) but *we did make money!* And we only picked our dogs
because we thought they had kind faces or pretty names, or because we had a sort of intimation—prompting—a sort of intuition, don't you know. The dog with a kind face came in second,
and looked so happy, the dear. The dog with a pretty name won,

easily, and always looked the winner, although it was a rank outsider. The dog about which we had intuitions finished last, of course.

I did not find the atmosphere exciting. The great crowd never seemed to fuse into a single entity, like a football crowd, for instance, or a theatre audience. There was a minimum of corporate excitement. There was no great cheering at the end of the race. I could feel no strong tension during a race, nor any powerful expectancy before one.

The promoters do little to make the spectacular side, the drama, of the race exciting. There is a parade of the competitors, but no one seems to bother very much about it. Loudspeakers uttered a recorded and unimpressive fanfare, and six young women—no, young ladies—led six pooches slowly round the track. The dogs wore muzzles and the gals wore velvet tam-o'shanters, slacks, not very clean dusters and looked as though they had wandered out of a touring production of *La Bohème*. They all seemed bored and the whole proceeding attracted a minimum of attention.

A note of color, as they say, is struck by each dog wearing a little flannel saddle, one white, one black, one red, one blue, one orange and one striped. That's to enable you to distinguish the dog you've backed from the others. You aren't expected to know one dog from another; but you are, oddly enough, expected to know black from white.

The dogs are shut up in traps, each with a gate that flies open when the judge gives the signal to start. Then the electric hare is started. That's quite nice because it makes a rather thrilling whirring noise, like a very, very expensive toy train, and simply flies along. By the pace it sets, you suddenly realize that the dogs must be able to run very fast indeed. Incidentally, I think it's very decent and obedient of the dogs to chase such an object, because it wouldn't deceive a child of three. It's just like an old fur glove on a wire. I suppose it smells of rabbit, but it couldn't look more crummy. Well, then, the dogs run after the thing and one of them comes in first, and there's a lot of expensive apparatus to photograph the finish in case the decision is queried. Then the judge, a spotlighted figure in the glass box, stands up and raises his bowler hat in token of something or other—homage, perhaps, to the victorious quadruped. And then you get on with the serious business of collecting your dough and staking money on the next race.

Maybe the night I was there was exceptional. I don't pretend to generalize, I'm only reporting what I saw. But there was no outward excitement, no hilarity, no sense of occasion. It was just a great, well-organized, polite business routine. We might just as well have been on the Stock Exchange. Instead of backing Burma Oil or Consolidated Nickel we backed greyhounds in flannel saddles. Maybe you'll think I'm a prig and a puritan, but it struck me as a sordid, decadent and deplorable carry-on. Naturally I knew that there must have been people present who were really interested in the sport, as opposed to the mere money side. I come from a part of Ireland where greyhounds are one of our chief exports, where their points and form are an endless topic of interest and debate. But—naturally, this is only a personal impression though gathered, all the same, from carefully observed evidence—I could not feel that there were many sportsmen present. To the vast majority of us the evening represented six little spots of financial excitement, six little spots of greedy hope, six little lights in the darkness, like the cigarette stubs burning in the dusk.

Certainly there's no cruelty involved. But I found myself wondering whether even that wasn't rather decadent; whether the instinct that wants to see blood flow, that just wants to see life and limb risked isn't more robust and vital than this sanitary, polite, monetary transaction. We queued at windows and booked tickets, bought tickets, changed money. We listlessly watched animals chase a bit of mechanism and I'm convinced that not one in a thousand of those present would have objected if the dogs, too, had been mechanized. Then we queued again at a window and again money changed hands—tinkling, jingling money, rustling, crinkling money, big money, real money, lovely, lovely money.

I don't think anyone would have been very pleased if the money had been mechanized, and if the pleasant ladies at the windows had suddenly passed out electric fur gloves that merely smelt like money.

Totalizator—Tote—isn't that very word like a knell? Make no mistake about it, the Tote—that miracle of flying wheels and cogs and calculations—dominates the track as a judge dominates a law court, as the sun dominates the heavens. And this man-made Lord of the Race Course, fascinating and intricate, though it very nearly has a brain, has no equivalent to a heart.

Of all the sporting events that I have ever seen this was the most entirely loveless.

Boxing

As in other parts of Europe, and in the United States, boxing is also popular in England.

The National Boxing Championship of the Army Cadet Force Association which I attended took place at the Albert Hall, in London, and quite a large audience was present. One felt however that the event was not primarily designed to please the audience. It was more a contest of skill. It can be said, of course, that this is also true of football matches or greyhound races. Certainly they may have been this originally, and still may be—sometimes. But the football and the dog racing which I attended were primarily pieces of commercial promotion and only secondarily displays of skill and sportsmanship.

At the Albert Hall the audience was of quite another character. To begin with, nearly all were soldiers in uniform; it quite clearly was not the commercial prizefight audience. On the other hand, I don't think it was an audience that by and large knew very much about boxing. One had no feeling, as I

had at the Brass Band Festival at Bolton, that an expert audience was alertly following the course of events. The audience
at the Albert Hall felt rather listless—to say bored would be
putting it too strongly—but the spiritual climate was more
wholesome than exciting. I, for one, did not find it bracing.
I think there were two particular reasons for this: first, the
Albert Hall is far too big; the entertainment was a half pint in
a ten gallon pot—and that's wholly inimical to excitement.
Second, a devastating mistake was made in showmanship. I am
fully aware that showmanship was largely irrelevant, and I
really don't see how the mistake could have been avoided. But
all the same the effect on the occasion was crashing.

Just as the first contest was about to begin, a young officer
got up into the ring and reminded us all, by loudspeaker, that
under the rules of the competition, applause or reaction from
the audience was permissible between rounds, but forbidden
during rounds. One sees perfectly sound reasons for such a rule.
In a small hall and an intimate atmosphere we could have been
reminded of it without such injury to the occasion. But something a shade tactless in the voice on the microphone, a subtle
and probably quite unintentional effect of superiority, a reminder that this was a military occasion and an order was
being given, that an officer was speaking to men, a grown-up to
adolescents—all this, combined with the echoing dim vast melan-
choly of a not-quite-full Albert Hall cast a chill over the occasion.

There was a particularly good moment when the house-
lights went out for the first time and emphasis was suddenly
thrown upon the ring—brilliantly white, blazing in the rays of
thirteen powerful focus lamps—with white ropes and white
floor. It looked like a place of execution. Silence. A small bell.
Then two tiny little boys in white shorts clambered up into the
lighted area. They must have been fifteen, but were very small.
The immensity of the surroundings diminished them still more.
It was rather touching to see the zeal—and the skill—with which
the two set about one another.

Throughout the contest one was impressed by its sportsmanship. It was a display of courage and skill and energy; aggressive impulses were being expressed with perfectly good temper and under the control of an agreed set of conventions. The bell would clang and two youths who, a split second before, had been going for each other with might and main, like tigers, like little aggressive engines, would stop dead, smile at one another, put their arms around each other and leave the ring locked together in perfect amity. If only, one couldn't help thinking, the Queensberry Rules could be applied to war, or even commercial affairs, or even bargain sales. But then, if they could, we should have to put up with the equivalent of the schoolmastery voice on the microphone.

Which do we want? The sane, sanitary, reasonable, disciplined but rather rigid, arid organization of contest? Or the prize ring with its slap-happy, bloodlusting, bawling, yelling audiences, with lots of cigar smoke and spittle, and blood on the floor, and a sinister, constant chink of money in the background?

Which?

For at the present stage of human development we keep having—and not just in sports—to face the choice, or else try to work out a suitable compromise.

A Royal Occasion

Some years ago, when George VI was King of England, I was present at the annual parade of King's Scouts. These are the elite of the Boy Scout movement, a thousand picked from several hundred thousand to attend a special service in St. George's Chapel, Windsor, preceded on this occasion by a March Past at which the King took the salute at Windsor Castle.

It was a delicious spring afternoon, sunny and warm. Windsor looked lovely with flowers everywhere—daffodils, aubretia, yellow alyssum, cherries in white and pink, and the deeper pink of the crab. The March Past occurred in the quadrangle of the castle, a great big square with a lawn in the center and a gravel drive all around. The buildings of this part of the castle are, to my mind, ugly enough: Regency Gothic with a lot of artificial medievalism—rather like those fortresses we used to see in the windows of expensive toy shops. Still, in the glow of this spring afternoon, it looked suitably mellow, suitably imposing, suitably "in character" as a royal residence. Drawn up on the grass were about a hundred men and—I think I counted right—three women. These were Scout Commissioners and special guests who were privileged to meet Their Majesties before the March Past. Around the sides of the gravel drive were about another hundred of miscellaneous spectators. Most of them looked as though they might be the moms and dads of those who were about to march past.

In one corner was a group of handicapped Scouts, that is, Scouts who are blind or crippled or otherwise disabled. A good many of these must, I think, have been victims of infantile paralysis. They had thin little legs in irons, one or two were in wheelchairs, and two were carried flat on their backs in litters—spinal trouble, I suppose.

Well, bang, slap on the appointed hour, King George, Queen Elizabeth and Princess Margaret appeared to greet the privileged hundred and three on the grass. No fuss, no pomposity or grandeur whatsoever. They were just an ordinary husband and wife and daughter, pleasantly fulfilling a social engagement in their own home on a Sunday afternoon after lunch. They were even dressed as an idealization of the ordinary family party: the King in a gray suit with a bowler hat, the Queen in a blue coat and hat, and Princess Margaret in a sort of pinkish outfit. They could have passed completely without comment anywhere. And yet, their very ordinariness was effective—even touching. These, we all knew, were the same human beings, who, on occasion—jewelled, crowned, sceptred, bowing right, bowing left—go jogging, smiling, waving past, in glass coaches flanked by glittering horsemen: images, symbols, painted but living pictures of royalty, symbolic heads of the national family, symbolic Father and symbolic Mother—symbolic mom and dad.

It is not my business here to discuss the significance or the value of such symbols. Quite clearly they are profoundly significant, and, in my view, profoundly valuable. The relevant point here, I think, is that these three were the audience for the event that followed, and their presence gave to the ceremony a very particular quality. It is nice to play soldiers, and red Indians with our brothers and sisters, even with the children from next door; it's nicer still with an audience. But nicest of all is when the audience is Father and Mother—Look Mummy! Look Daddy! Look what *I'm* doing.

By now the last of the hundred and three hands were being shaken, and a band coming nearer and nearer announced the arrival of the thousand King's Scouts who were to march past. And now it was the turn of the handicapped Scouts to be greeted. Then, with an experienced minimum of fuss—the King and Queen just happened to be standing at the right place—through a gateway flanked by bogus fortified keeps, there swept the band of the Welsh Guards, tooting and thumping out one of those Flower Show Marches, and after them the thousand marchers, three by three by three.

King's Scouts are those who have reached the highest attainments in scouting. The Marchers Past were soggy with badges. They had passed, it was clear, through ordeal after ordeal, after test, after examination, after test, after ordeal. This was the company of the elect—and by St. George! they looked it. Not that they all looked like film stars, like heroes—they didn't. Lots of them were at the pimply stage, and lots wore very thick specs.

And there were lots of senior Scouts—boys of fifty summers —looking decidedly absurd in their shorts and wide-brimmed boyish hats. But individual absurdity only made the total effect more impressive. These stoutish elderly boys knew their stuff. That was the point. They could tie the right knots, shin up monkey-puzzlers, swim out to the wreck. They had given up, and were still giving up, time and energy to the movement, to something outside themselves, to something larger, more important than their own lives, their own careers.

I couldn't help comparing this ceremonial with the ceremonial side of the other public occasions I had attended—the ceremonial on the football ground and the dog track for instance.

Maybe one was comparing chalk with cheese. I don't know.

There are, I think, legitimate points of comparison. And one thing seems to emerge: audiences vary not only in quantity but quality. The good spectator is not passive; he does participate in, does help to create the occasion.

One remembers that little group in the corner of the quadrangle. I see again a blind boy having the scene described to him by another Scout, those pale little eager figures in the wheelchairs, who were none the less participants in the event. Handicapped they surely were, but still Scouts.

All honor to them, all honor to the imaginative sympathy that makes possible their full inclusion in the Scout idea.

And—look out! there's a moral coming—if, whether from necessity or choice, we find ourselves spectators at an event, don't let us be merely passive spectators, or money-makers on the side. Let us be participants. Let us, for goodness' gracious sake, be active in whatever event is afoot.